C

fulfilling life

Windy Dryden

Hodder Education

Hodder Education is an Hachette UK company

First published in UK 2012 by Hodder Education

First published in US 2012 by The McGraw-Hill Companies, Inc.

This edition published 2012.

Copyright © 2012 Windy Dryden

The publisher has used its best endeavours to ensure that any website addresses referred to in this
book are correct and active at the time of going to press. However, the publisher and the author have
no responsibility for the websites and can make no guarantee that a site will remain live or that the
content will remain relevant, decent or appropriate.

The publisher has made every effort to mark as such all words which it believes to be trademarks.
The publisher should also like to make it clear that the presence of a word in the book, whether
marked or unmarked, in no way affects its legal status as a trademark.

Every reasonable effort has been made by the publisher to trace the copyright holders of material in
this book. Any errors or omissions should be notified in writing to the publisher, who will endeavour
to rectify the situation for any reprints and future editions.

Hachette UK's policy is to use papers that are natural, renewable and recyclable products and made
from wood grown in sustainable forests. The logging and manufacturing processes are expected to
conform to the environmental regulations of the country of origin.

www.hoddereducation.co.uk

Typeset by Cenveo Publisher Services

Printed in Great Britain

Also available
in ebook

Contents

1

what is rational emotive behaviour therapy (REBT)?

Cognitive Behaviour Therapy (CBT) is a major tradition within the field of counselling and psychotherapy and this tradition comprises several different approaches. This book is based on the longest established approach to CBT known as Rational Emotive Behaviour Therapy (REBT) founded in the mid 1950s by the American psychologist, Dr. Albert Ellis (1913–2007). In this opening chapter I will consider the four words that make up the approach's name: rational, emotive, behaviour and therapy as a way of introducing you to this CBT approach. I will start by discussing what the terms 'rational' and 'irrational' mean as they relate to beliefs, a core concept in REBT. I will then show how REBT conceives of emotion and behaviour. Finally, I will review the three levels of therapy that REBT addresses – disturbance, dissatisfaction and development – and explain why REBT recommends that you tackle such problems in that order.

In the field of counselling and psychotherapy today, much attention is being focused on a therapeutic tradition known as Cognitive Behaviour Therapy (which I will refer to as CBT). In my view, CBT is a therapeutic tradition rather than a therapeutic approach because there are, in fact, many approaches that come under the umbrella of CBT. While there are differences among these approaches, they all share the view that our emotional problems are closely linked to how we think about ourselves, others and the world and how we act based on such thinking. All this goes back to the early Stoic philosophers, one of whom, Epictetus, said: 'People are disturbed not by things, but by their views of things.'

One of these CBT approaches is known as Rational Emotive Behaviour Therapy (henceforth called REBT), which is the focus of this book. It is the approach I am going to use to show you how you can think rationally so that you can be emotionally healthy in the face of life's adversities. Thus, while the title highlights the therapeutic tradition, this book is based on a specific approach within this tradition. In this opening chapter I will discuss in turn the four words that comprise the therapy's name as a way of explaining what REBT is and what its major focus is.

The terms 'rational' and 'irrational' in current REBT theory are most commonly used as adjectives in front of the noun 'beliefs'.

Let me consider the major characteristics of rational beliefs and contrast these with the major characteristics of irrational beliefs. In what follows, I will consider the rational belief in the left-hand column and the irrational belief in the right-hand column to facilitate the comparison.

A rational belief is flexible or non-extreme	An irrational belief is rigid or extreme
1 A rational belief is flexible	**1 An irrational belief is rigid**
Here is an example of a rational belief that is flexible: *'I want my colleague to like me, but she does not have to do so.'*	Here is an example of an irrational belief that is rigid: *'My colleague has to like me.'*

A rational belief is flexible or non-extreme	An irrational belief is rigid or extreme
Imagine that you hold such a belief. As you do so, you will see that this belief is flexible because while you assert what you want (i.e. *'I want my colleague to like me...'*), you also acknowledge that you do not have to get what you want (i.e. *'...but she does not have to do so'*).	To compare this belief with the flexible version in the left-hand column, we need to state it in its full form: *'I want my colleague to like me, therefore she has to do so.'* Again, imagine that you hold this belief. As you do so, you will see that this belief is rigid because, while you not only assert what you want (i.e. *'I want my colleague to like me...'*), you also demand that you have to get it *(i.e. '...therefore she has to do so')*.

2 A rational belief is non-extreme

Here is an example of a rational belief that is non-extreme:

'It is bad if my colleague does not like me, but not the end of the world.'

Again imagine that you hold this belief. As you do so, you will see that this belief is non-extreme because, while you assert that you find the event negative (i.e. *'It is bad if my colleague does not like me...'*),

2 An irrational belief is extreme

Here is an example of an irrational belief that is extreme:

'It is the end of the world if my colleague does not like me.'

To compare it to the non-extreme version in the left-hand column we need to state it in its full form:
'It is bad if my colleague does not like me, and therefore it is the end of the world.'

(Contd)

A rational belief is flexible or non-extreme	An irrational belief is rigid or extreme
you also acknowledge that such an evaluation is not extreme because it could always be worse (i.e. '...*but not the end of the world*').	Again imagine that you hold this belief. As you do so you will see that this belief is extreme because you not only assert that you find the event negative (i.e. '*It is bad if my colleague does not like me...* '), you also claim that it could not be worse (i.e. '...*and therefore it is the end of the world*').

A rational belief is true	An irrational belief is false
Imagine that you hold the following rational belief that I introduced above: '*I want my colleague to like me, but she does not have to do so.*' You will note that this belief is made up of two parts: * '*I want my colleague to like me...*' * '*...but she does not have to do so.*' Let's take one part at a time. First, you can prove that you would like your colleague to like you; after all this is your desire. Also, you can probably cite reasons why you want your colleague to like you	Now imagine that you hold the following irrational belief that I introduced above: '*My colleague has to like me.*' Again this belief is made up of two parts: * '*I want my colleague to like me...*' * '*...and therefore she has to do so.*' Let's take one part at a time. First, you can again prove that you would like the other person to like you for reasons discussed opposite. So, the first part of your belief is true.

A rational belief is true	An irrational belief is false
(e.g. it makes for a good working relationship where you can help each other). So, the first part of your belief is true.	Now let's look at the second part of the irrational belief. You cannot prove that your colleague has to like you. If that were true, she would have no choice but to like you. This demanding component of your irrational belief in effect robs your colleague of free choice, which she retains in the face of your demand. Thus, this second part is false.
Now let's look at the second part of the rational belief. You can also prove that the other person does not have to like you. To state otherwise would be to deny that person free choice.	
So if both parts of this rational belief are true then we can say that the belief taken as a whole is true.	As both parts of a belief have to be true for the belief to be true then we can say that the irrational belief is false. Also, when we consider this irrational belief in its short form (i.e. 'My colleague has to like me'), then it is clear that it is false since it again attempts to rob your colleague of the freedom not to like you which she does in reality have.

A rational belief is sensible	An irrational belief is not sensible
Taking the rational belief 'I want my colleague to like me, but she does not have to do so', we can ask the question: does this belief make sense?	Taking the full form of your irrational belief 'I want my colleague to like me, and therefore she has to do so', we can again ask the question: *(Contd)*

A rational belief is sensible	An irrational belief is not sensible
We can answer that it does since you are explicitly acknowledging that there is no connection between what you want and what you have to get.	does this belief make sense? Here our answer is that it does not because it asserts that there is a connection between what you want and what you have to get. The idea that because you want something you have to get it is, in fact, childish nonsense when coming from an adult.

A rational belief is largely constructive	An irrational belief is largely unconstructive
When you hold a rational belief the consequences of doing so will be largely constructive. For example, let's suppose that you hold the rational belief, '*I want my colleague to like me, but she does not have to do so*', and you bring this belief to a situation where your colleague snaps at you for no good reason. In this situation you will experience three different, but related, consequences which I will now illustrate:	When you hold an irrational belief the consequences of doing so will be largely unconstructive. For example, let's suppose that you hold the irrational belief, '*My colleague must like me*', and you bring this belief to the situation where your colleague snaps at you for no good reason. In this situation you will experience three different, but related, consequences which I will now illustrate. As I do so, compare these consequences to those that stem from your belief if it were rational (see opposite):

A rational belief is largely constructive	An irrational belief is largely unconstructive
1 **Emotional consequence** Here you will tend to be concerned about your colleague's response, but not anxious about it.	1 **Emotional consequence** Here you will tend to be anxious, rather than concerned, about your colleague's response.
2 **Behavioural consequence** Here you will be likely to enquire of your colleague in an open way if there is anything wrong.	2 **Behavioural consequence** Here you will tend to avoid your colleague or try desperately to get her to like you.
3 **Thinking consequence** Here you will tend to think that your colleague is upset with someone or something which could be to do with you, but may well be nothing to do with you.	3 **Thinking consequence** Here you will tend to think that your colleague is upset with you rather than with someone or something that had nothing to do with you.

Emotive

The term 'emotive' in REBT means that which is relevant to your emotions. Like every other approach to therapy, REBT is based on a model of emotions. Since REBT is a therapeutic approach it is primarily concerned with relieving people's emotional disturbance. However, it also acknowledges that people are bound to have negative emotions when faced with negative life events (henceforth called adversities in this book). To accommodate these two positions REBT distinguishes between emotions that are negative in tone and have largely unconstructive consequences and emotions that are negative in tone and have largely constructive consequences. The former are known as unhealthy negative emotions (UNEs) and the latter healthy negative emotions (HNEs).

The REBT model of emotion states that the emotions that we experience are based largely on the beliefs that we hold about ourselves, others and the world. More specifically it states that our unhealthy negative emotions about life's adversities are based largely on the irrational beliefs that we hold about these adversities and that, if we want to experience healthy negative emotions about the adversities in question, we need to change our irrational beliefs to rational beliefs.

Because these adversities are negative, it is not appropriate for you to feel good about them or even neutral about them. It is healthy to experience negative emotions, but not problematic ones, about such life events. These problematic emotions in REBT are unhealthy negative emotions (UNEs) and these are listed in Table 1.1 and contrasted with their healthy negative equivalents (HNEs).

Table 1.1 Unhealthy negative emotions and their healthy alternatives.

Unhealthy negative emotions	Healthy negative emotions[1]
Anxiety	Concern
Depression	Sadness
Guilt	Remorse
Shame	Disappointment
Hurt	Sorrow
Unhealthy anger	Healthy anger
Unhealthy jealousy	Healthy jealousy
Unhealthy envy	Healthy envy

[1]We do not have commonly agreed words in the English language to describe healthy negative emotions. The terms that I have used in the right-hand column of the above table are my own. Feel free to use alternative terms that are more meaningful to you.

The term 'behaviour' in REBT refers to both overt behaviour and to an urge to act that is not translated into overt behaviour. The latter is known as an action tendency. REBT's model of behaviour parallels its model of emotions in arguing that irrational beliefs tend to lead to behaviour that is largely unconstructive in effect and that rational beliefs lead to behaviour that is largely constructive in effect. The former is associated with unhealthy negative emotions (UNEs) and the latter with healthy negative emotions (HNEs).

In Table 1.2 I outline the major behaviours associated with the eight unhealthy and healthy negative emotions listed above.

Table 1.2 The major behaviours associated with the eight unhealthy and healthy negative emotions.

Unhealthy negative emotion with associated unconstructive behaviours and action tendencies	Healthy negative emotion with associated constructive behaviours and action tendencies
Anxiety * Withdrawing from threat * Avoiding threat * Seeking reassurance even though not reassurable * Seeking safety from threat	**Concern** * Confronting threat * Seeking reassurance when reassurable
Depression * Prolonged withdrawal from enjoyable activities	**Sadness** * Engaging with enjoyable activities after a period of mourning or adjustment to the loss
Guilt * Begging for forgiveness	**Remorse** * Asking, not begging, for forgiveness

Unhealthy negative emotion with associated unconstructive behaviours and action tendencies	Healthy negative emotion with associated constructive behaviours and action tendencies
Shame * Withdrawing from others * Avoiding eye contact with others	**Disappointment** * Keeping in contact with others * Maintaining eye contact with others
Hurt * Sulking	**Sorrow** * Assertion and communicating with others
Unhealthy anger * Aggression (direct and indirect)	**Healthy anger** * Assertion
Unhealthy jealousy * Prolonged suspicious questioning of the other person * Checking on the other * Restricting the other	**Healthy jealousy** * Brief, open-minded questioning of the other person * Not checking on the other * Not restricting the other
Unhealthy envy * Spoiling the other's enjoyment of the desired possession	**Healthy envy** * Striving to gain a similar possession for oneself if it is truly what you want

The behaviours listed in Table 1.2 are what a person does or tends to do when her irrational or rational belief about an adversity has been fully activated. However, the impact of belief on behaviour can be seen in other ways.

Short-term self-protective behaviour

In the 'ABC' model that I have presented in this chapter, an adversity occurs or is deemed to occur at 'A', the person holds a belief about this adversity at 'B' and experiences emotional, behavioural and thinking consequences of holding this belief at 'C'. In this model the person's belief (e.g. 'My colleague must like me') is specific to the specific adversity that she encounters.

However, beliefs can be held at a more general level (e.g. 'People with whom I work must like me') and, when a belief is more general in nature, the person has a tendency to bring such a belief with them, as it were, to situations where a relevant adversity may occur. Thus, in our example, if a person holds a general irrational belief (e.g. 'People with whom I work must like me'), then the person will be hypersensitive to the possibility of not being liked by a colleague and act to prevent this adversity actually occurring (e.g. by being extra nice to a person whom she thinks may show, but has not yet shown, some disapproval of her). In this way the person is acting to protect herself in the short-term, but the longer-term effect of this behaviour is unconstructive in a number of ways:

* she does not get to test out her hunch that the person will disapprove of her
* she does not get to deal constructively with such disapproval should it occur and
* she tends to maintain her irrational belief since she is acting in a way that is consistent with it.

Overcompensatory behaviour

When a person holds an irrational belief and particularly one that is general in nature, then she may try to deal with actual or potential adversities by behaving in a manner that is overcompensatory. By using overcompensatory behaviour the person is trying to prove to herself the opposite of what she actually thinks is the truth about her, the other person or the world. A common example of this occurs when a person privately considers that he would be weak if he can't deal with a challenge, but tries to prove to himself that he is strong by facing an even greater challenge.

The word 'therapy' comes from the Greek *therapeia* meaning 'a service, an attendance' which, in turn, is related to the Greek verb *therapeuo* meaning 'I wait upon'.

REBT therapists, therefore, can be seen to offer a 'service' to people who have problems in a number of areas:

1 emotional problems
2 practical, dissatisfaction problems *and*
3 personal development problems.

A distinctive feature of REBT is that it outlines a logical order for dealing with these problems.

Disturbance before dissatisfaction

REBT argues that, unless there are good reasons to the contrary, it is best for us to address our emotional problems before our dissatisfaction problems. The reasoning is as follows. If we try and deal with our dissatisfaction before we deal with our emotional disturbance, then our disturbed feelings will get in the way of our efforts to change directly the adversities about which we are dissatisfied.

Disturbance before development

In the late 1960s and early 1970s I used to go to a number of encounter groups. This was the era of personal growth or development. However, there were a number of casualties of these groups and when these occurred it was because attendees were preoccupied with issues of emotional disturbance and they were being pushed too hard to go into areas of development that warranted greater resilience.

In general, then, it is very difficult for us to develop ourselves when we are emotionally disturbed. To focus on areas of development when someone is emotionally disturbed is akin to encouraging that person to climb a very steep hill with very heavy weights attached to their ankles. First help the person to remove their ankle weights (i.e. address their emotional disturbance) before discussing the best way of climbing the hill!

Dissatisfaction before development

Abraham Maslow (1968) is perhaps best known for his work on self-actualization. The relevance of this concept for our present discussion is this. It is very difficult for humans to focus on higher-order 'needs' when we are preoccupied with issues with respect to lower-order needs. Thus, if a person is faced with a general dissatisfying life experience which cannot be compartmentalized and also wants to explore his writing ambitions, he should address the former first – unless this life dissatisfaction will help him write a better book!

I have outlined REBT's preferred order in dealing with problems; it also values flexibility. Thus, if a person wants to deal with his problems in a different order, he should do so and observe the results. If it works, that is fine. If not, then REBT's preferred position may prove to yield better results. The proof of the pudding is in the eating!

Now that I have discussed the four terms that make up the name of the therapy, in the next chapter I will consider REBT's famous ABC model in much greater detail.

2

understanding the 'Situational ABC' framework

CBT is a therapeutic tradition which values explicitness and specificity and these qualities are in evidence when REBT explains your responses to life's events. The framework that REBT employs to help you do this is known as the 'Situational ABC' model. In this chapter, I will discuss the four components of this model. You experience emotions and behaviours at 'C' about a key aspect of the situation that you are in. This key aspect is known as an 'activating event' (or 'A'). REBT's main point is that your responses at 'C' are not due to 'A' but largely to the beliefs ('B') that you hold about 'A'. When 'A' is an adversity and you are disturbed about it, this is largely due to the set of irrational beliefs that you hold about 'A'. In order to respond healthily to this adversity, you need to hold a set of rational beliefs.

Every approach to counselling and psychotherapy is based on a framework which explains emotional problems and suggests solutions to these problems. REBT is based on a 'Situational ABC' framework which I will discuss in this chapter.

The 'situation'

When you have an emotional problem, you actually experience this problem in specific situations. As we will see, in REBT we recommend analysing these situations one at a time. So, when you take an example of your emotional problem, you will need to begin by describing the situation in which the problem occurred. When you describe the situation, remember the 'four Ws' – where, when, who and what:

Where you were
When you were there
Who else was present
What happened

'A' – the adversity

In REBT, 'A' stands for the aspect of the situation to which the person responds with an unhealthy negative emotion and unconstructive behaviour, for example. In this book, I will call this the 'adversity'. I will discuss how to assess 'A' in Chapter 5.

The most important thing to understand about 'A' is that it is an inference (also known as an interpretation) about what is going on. An inference is a hunch about reality which may be true or false, but goes beyond the data at hand.

'B' – beliefs

Epictetus, the Roman slave philosopher, is credited with the following saying: 'People are disturbed not by things, but by their views of things.' This is the essence of Cognitive Behaviour Therapy. In REBT, which you will recall is a specific approach within the CBT tradition, these 'views' are known as beliefs. The REBT version of the Epictetus saying is this: 'People are not disturbed by things; rather, they disturb themselves when they hold irrational beliefs about things. When they hold rational beliefs, they respond healthily to things.'

As shown above, REBT theory distinguishes between two types of beliefs: irrational beliefs and rational beliefs. Furthermore, this theory argues that irrational beliefs explain why people have emotional problems about adversities and rational beliefs explain why they have healthy responses to the same adversities.

I will describe irrational beliefs first.

Irrational beliefs

Irrational beliefs are so-called because they have a number of characteristics as first discussed in Chapter 1. They are rigid or extreme, not reality-based, not sensible or logical, and they tend to lead to unhealthy consequences.

In REBT, there are two types of irrational beliefs: rigid beliefs and extreme beliefs. Rigid beliefs are regarded as primary and extreme beliefs (of which there are three) are seen as secondary conclusions from these primary beliefs.

Rigid beliefs

When you hold a rigid belief you not only outline what you want to happen (or don't want to happen), you demand that it *must* happen (or that it *must not* happen). Rigid beliefs take the form of 'musts', 'absolute shoulds', 'have-tos', 'got-tos', etc.

Extreme beliefs

As the name implies, when you hold an extreme belief, you are being extreme in your judgement of yourself, other people or life conditions. In REBT there are three extreme beliefs.

Awfulizing beliefs

When you hold an awfulizing belief you are being extreme in your judgement of an adversity. You are not just saying that it is bad that the adversity has occurred, you are saying that it is awful that it happened. Awfulizing beliefs take the form of 'it's awful that...', 'it's terrible that...' and 'it's the end of the world that...'.

Discomfort intolerance beliefs

When an adversity happens at 'A', and you hold a discomfort intolerance belief, you are extreme in your judgement of your ability to tolerate the adversity. You not only indicate that it is difficult to tolerate the adversity, you hold that you can't tolerate it. Discomfort intolerance beliefs take the form of 'I can't bear it...', 'I can't stand it...' and 'it's intolerable...'.

Depreciation beliefs

You can hold a depreciation belief about yourself, about another person or about life conditions. When you do so, you are extreme in your judgement to the extent that you apply a global negative judgement to yourself (e.g. 'I'm worthless'), to the other person (e.g. 'You are a bad person') or to life conditions (e.g. 'Life is bad').

Rational beliefs

Rational beliefs are so-called because they have a number of characteristics that I first discussed in Chapter 1. They are flexible or non-extreme, reality-based, sensible or logical and they tend to lead to healthy consequences.

In REBT, there are two types of rational beliefs: flexible beliefs and non-extreme beliefs. Flexible beliefs are regarded as primary and non-extreme beliefs (of which there are three) are seen as secondary conclusions from these primary beliefs.

Flexible beliefs

When you hold a flexible belief you outline what you want to happen (or don't want to happen), but you do not demand that it *must* happen (or that it *must not* happen). Flexible beliefs take the form of 'preferences', 'preferential shoulds', 'desires', 'wishes', 'wants', etc. However, a defining characteristic of such flexible beliefs is a full acknowledgement that you do not have to get what you prefer, etc.

Non-extreme beliefs

As the name implies, when you hold a non-extreme belief, you are being non-extreme or relative in your judgement of yourself, other people or life conditions. In REBT there are three non-extreme beliefs.

Non-awfulizing beliefs

When you hold a non-awfulizing belief you are being relative in your judgement of an adversity. You are saying that it is bad, but not awful, that the adversity has occurred. Non-awfulizing beliefs take the form of 'it's bad that...', 'it's unfortunate that...' and 'it's troublesome that...'. However, a defining characteristic of such non-awfulizing beliefs is a full acknowledgement that it is not terrible, awful or the end of the world if the adversity occurs.

Discomfort tolerance beliefs

When you encounter an adversity at 'A' and you hold a discomfort tolerance belief about it you are being relative or non-extreme in your judgement of your ability to tolerate the adversity. You accept that, while it is difficult to tolerate the adversity, you can tolerate it and it is worth it to you to do so.

Discomfort tolerance beliefs take the form of 'I can put up with it...', 'I can stand it...' and 'it's tolerable...'. However, a defining characteristic of such discomfort tolerance beliefs is a full acknowledgement that it is worth it to you to bear the adversity, not just that you can do so.

Unconditional acceptance beliefs

You can hold an unconditional acceptance belief about yourself, about another person or about life conditions. When you do so you are again being non-extreme in your judgement to the extent that this acknowledges the complexity, fallibility and fluidity of a person and the complexity and fluidity of life conditions. This judgement is unconditional in nature which means that it remains the same no matter what you do, what the other person does or what happens in life.

It is important to point out that when you hold an unconditional acceptance belief this does not preclude you from making a judgement of an aspect of yourself, of the other person or of life conditions. However, it does mean that you refrain from judging the whole of you, the whole of the other person or the whole of life on the basis of that specific and focused evaluation.

If we look at an unconditional self-acceptance belief, for example, this takes the form of 'I am fallible...', 'I am a unique person...', 'I am acceptable because I am alive...'. However, the defining characteristic of such beliefs is a full acknowledgement that such views are unconditional.

Similar points can be made with reference to an unconditional other-acceptance belief and to an unconditional life-acceptance belief.

'C' – consequences of beliefs about 'A'

In REBT there are three major consequences of beliefs: emotional, behavioural and thinking consequences. In this section, I will begin by considering the consequences of holding irrational beliefs and then I will consider the consequences of holding rational beliefs.

Consequences of holding irrational beliefs

When people hold rigid and extreme beliefs about adversities at 'A', they will experience three main problematic and unconstructive consequences. I will deal with these one at a time.

Emotional consequences

When people come for counselling it is usually because they are in some kind of emotional pain. As I first explained in Chapter 1, REBT argues that it is important to distinguish between unhealthy negative emotions (UNEs) and healthy negative emotions (HNEs). As the term makes clear, unhealthy negative emotions are those emotions that are negative in tone and unhealthy in effects. When you encounter an adversity, it is important to remember that this is a negative event. It is therefore to be expected that your emotional response will be negative in tone. It is not healthy for you to feel nothing about a negative event, nor is it healthy for you to have a positive emotion about a negative event. So what makes an emotion unhealthy is not that it is negative in tone, but that it is unhealthy in its consequences.

In Chapter 1, I presented a list of the eight major unhealthy negative emotions for which people seek counselling help. Here is a reminder of these emotions: anxiety, depression, guilt, shame, hurt, unhealthy anger, unhealthy jealousy and unhealthy envy.

Behavioural consequences

When you hold irrational beliefs about an adversity, these beliefs will tend to lead you to behave in a largely unconstructive manner. Behavioural consequences of irrational beliefs may be expressed as overt behaviour or as a tendency to act in a certain way which you may or may not transform into actual behaviour. When your belief is irrational and it leads to unconstructive overt behaviour then you will physically do something (such as hit someone when your anger is problematic). However, when your beliefs are irrational, you may also feel like acting in an unhealthy way, but are able to suppress it. Thus, in unhealthy anger, you may feel like smashing another person in the face, although you don't do so. This is your action tendency that you don't transform into overt behaviour.

When your behaviour is unconstructive (either overt or intended, but not acted on), you tend to:

1 make unhealthy attempts to get rid of accompanying feelings
2 make impulsive attempts to change the adversity
3 make premature attempts to withdraw from the adversity
4 avoid the adversity when facing up to it would be indicated

    5 experience a negative impact on your relationships with relevant people

    6 experience interruptions to achieving your goals.

Thinking consequences

When you hold irrational beliefs about an adversity these beliefs will tend to lead you subsequently to think in highly distorted and negative ways.

These thoughts are usually inferences (or interpretations), but they differ from the inferences that you make at 'A' in that 'C' inferences are usually more distorted than 'A' inferences. This is because 'C' inferences are the outcome of irrational beliefs and 'A' inferences have not yet been processed by these beliefs.

Consequences of holding rational beliefs

When people hold flexible and non-extreme beliefs about adversities at 'A', they will experience three main healthy and constructive consequences. I will deal with these one at a time.

Emotional consequences

When people face adversities and hold rational beliefs about these adversities, they experience healthy negative emotions. As the term makes clear, healthy negative emotions are those emotions that are negative in tone and healthy in effects.

In Chapter 1, I presented a list of the eight major healthy negative emotions that are the alternatives to the eight major unhealthy negative emotions presented above that people seek counselling help for. Here is a reminder of these healthy negative emotions: concern (rather than anxiety), sadness (rather than depression), remorse (rather than guilt), disappointment (rather than shame), sorrow (rather than hurt), healthy anger (rather than unhealthy anger), healthy jealousy (rather than unhealthy jealousy) and healthy envy (rather than unhealthy envy).

As I noted in Chapter 1, as we have no agreed terms for healthy negative emotions, the terms used above are my own. Feel free to use your own terms if they are more meaningful to you.

Behavioural consequences

When you hold rational beliefs about an adversity these beliefs will tend to lead you to behave (overt actions and action tendencies) in a constructive manner.

When your behaviour is constructive (either overt or intended, but not acted on), you tend to:

1 make healthy attempts to deal with accompanying feelings
2 make considered attempts to change the adversity
3 remain in the presence of the adversity to deal with it rather than withdraw from it
4 face up to the adversity rather than avoid it
5 experience a positive impact on your relationships with relevant people
6 move closer to achieving your goals.

Thinking consequences

When you hold rational beliefs about an adversity these beliefs will tend to lead you subsequently to think in realistic and balanced ways.

In the next chapter I will provide an overview of how to tackle one of your problems using REBT.

tackling your
problems:
an overview

In this chapter, I provide an overview of the steps that you need to take in order to tackle your problems using CBT. I stress that it's best to tackle your problems one at a time and when you have selected one – known as a target problem – it is best to take a specific example of this target problem to work through using the 'Situational ABC' framework as you do so. After setting goals, you need to see that developing rational alternatives to your irrational beliefs will help you to achieve these goals. Questioning your beliefs will help you to understand why your irrational beliefs are irrational and why your rational beliefs are rational, and acting in ways that are consistent with the latter will help you to strengthen your conviction in them. As you work towards your goals you will experience lapses along the way which you need to address.

In this chapter I provide an overview of the steps that you will take when you use this book to tackle one of your emotional problems one at a time.

Step 1: Admit that you have an emotional problem

Unless you admit to yourself that you have an emotional problem, then you will obviously not do anything to help yourself, since you do not think that you need help. If you have an emotional problem, you will experience debilitating emotional pain accompanied by a sense of being stuck in a way of thinking, feeling and behaving which has an unhealthy effect on your life and interferes with you working towards your goals. If you have an emotional problem, then the main reason why you will not admit this to yourself is that you feel ashamed of having the problem. Shame, in this context, stems from the irrational belief that 'I must be strong and in control and I am a defective person if I am not'.

For you to admit that you have an emotional problem, therefore, you need to see that you are not a defective person for having the problem. Rather, you are an ordinary person who is not immune from having emotional problems. Developing this attitude will lead you to admit to having an emotional problem and to take the next step.

Step 2: Assess a specific example of your emotional problem

In order to tackle your emotional problem, you need to understand it. Taking a specific example of this problem is the best initial step you can take to do this. Then you need to use the 'Situational ABC' framework – discussed in Chapter 2 – to provide you with the necessary information to help you to address the problem in the following way:

* Describe the 'situation' in which your problem occurred.
* Identify 'C'. This will be the major problematic emotion you experienced in this situation along with what you did (or felt like doing) and your associated thinking.
* Identify your 'A'. Remember that 'A' stands for 'adversity' and will be the aspect of the situation about which you were most disturbed.
* Identify your irrational beliefs at 'B'. These will be a rigid belief and at least one extreme belief that, taken together, account for your responses at 'C' to 'A'. This step is particularly important because it helps you to understand that your emotional problem is not caused by the adversity. Rather, your emotional problem stems from the irrational beliefs that you hold *about* the adversity.

Step 3: Set goals

Once you have assessed the specific example of your problem, it is important that you have a clear idea of what constitutes a healthy way of responding to the same adversity at 'A'. Here, it is important that you choose a goal that is realistic and to which you can commit yourself. Ideally this goal should comprise healthy emotional, behavioural and thinking responses.

It is also important for you to see that these healthy responses are underpinned by alternative rational beliefs at 'B'. These beliefs will comprise a flexible belief (the healthy alternative to your rigid belief) and your main non-extreme belief (a healthy alternative to your main extreme belief).

Step 4: Identify your rational beliefs and see that these will help you to achieve your goals

Once you have set goals, you need to see that the best way to achieve these goals is to develop alternatives to the irrational beliefs that underpin your problems. This involves you:

* developing a flexible belief as an alternative to your rigid belief
* developing a non-extreme belief as an alternative to the extreme belief that, together with your rigid belief, was most responsible for your disturbance. If this was an awfulizing belief, develop a non-awfulizing belief; if it was a discomfort intolerance belief, develop a discomfort tolerance belief; and if it was a depreciation belief, develop the appropriate acceptance belief (see Chapter 2).

Once you have developed rational alternatives to your irrational beliefs, it is important that you understand that these will help you to achieve the goals that you specified in Step 3 above.

Step 5: Question your beliefs

Here, you need to question your irrational beliefs and your rational beliefs. The purpose of this questioning process is twofold:

1 First, it helps you to understand that your irrational beliefs are false, illogical and unhelpful in general and, more specifically, prevent you from achieving your goal of responding healthily to the adversity.

2 Second, it helps you to understand that your rational beliefs are true, logical and helpful in general and, more specifically, increase your chances of achieving your goal of responding healthily to the adversity.

Step 6: Strengthen your conviction in your rational beliefs and weaken your conviction in your irrational beliefs

Just understanding that your irrational beliefs are irrational (i.e. false, illogical and unhelpful) and that your rational beliefs are rational (true, logical and helpful) is usually not sufficient to change your irrational beliefs. In order to change these beliefs, it is important that you act and think in ways that are consistent with your developing rational beliefs and inconsistent with your currently held irrational beliefs.

You will need to commit yourself to this process of changing your beliefs until your feelings change to catch up with your healthy behaviour and thinking. To paraphrase Gandhi, you deal healthily with an adversity when there is consistency among your beliefs, behaviour, emotions and subsequent thinking with respect to the adversity.

Step 7: Generalize your learning

So far, I have discussed what you need to do in order to deal with a typical and specific example of your emotional problem. In order to generalize your learning you need to do two things:

1 Deal with other examples of your emotional problem when you encounter them using the same process of change that you employed in dealing with your selected typical and specific example.

2 Look for a general theme that appears in examples of your emotional problem. You will normally be able to find this when you look at 'A' in your 'Situational ABCs'. In Table 3.1 I list common themes that are associated with the eight major emotional problems for which people seek help.

Once you have found the theme, add your rigid demand and the major extreme belief that accounts for your problem and this becomes your core irrational belief. Then you need to develop an alternative core rational belief that comprises the theme plus a flexible belief and most appropriate non-extreme belief. Once you have done this you can use this core rational belief as a guide to think rationally as you face up to the adversities defined by the theme and act in ways that are

Table 3.1 Common themes associated with unhealthy negative emotions.

Theme of the adversity at 'A'	Emotional problem at 'C'
Threat	Anxiety
Loss / failure	Depression
Breaking your moral code; failing to live up to your moral code; hurting someone	Guilt
Falling very short of your ideal in a social context	Shame
Someone betrays you or lets you down and you think you do not deserve such treatment	Hurt
Self or other transgresses a personal rule; other threatens self-esteem; frustration	Unhealthy anger
Threat to valued relationship	Unhealthy jealousy
Others have what you value and lack	Unhealthy envy

consistent with this belief. I will deal with this topic in greater detail in Chapter 11.

Step 8: Dealing with lapses and relapse

Psychological change, like the course of true love, rarely runs smoothly. Having made progress we may take steps backwards and, if we do not deal with these lapses, we will relapse and go back to square one. If you accept that, at times, you will take steps back this will help you to learn from such lapses and as a result you will minimize the chances that you will relapse.

Another good way of minimizing the chances of relapse is to identify and deal with vulnerability factors. These are so called because they are factors that, if not dealt with, will mean that you are vulnerable to experiencing your problem. Such factors may be located in your environment (e.g. seeing other people smoking when you are trying to give up), to do with other people (e.g. people being rude to you when you are dealing with your need for approval) or to do with yourself (e.g. being bored when you are dealing with your tendency to overeat). If you can face up to these factors in a stepwise manner while rehearsing appropriate rational beliefs, then you will be successful at dealing with your vulnerability factors. I will deal with such issues in greater detail in Chapter 12.

Step 9: Deal with any distortions of 'A'

When you are dealing with a specific example of your problem, but normally after you have identified, challenged and changed your irrational beliefs, you need to revisit your adversity at 'A' to determine whether or not it was realistic or distorted. If your 'A' is distorted and you correct this distortion before you have identified and dealt with your irrational beliefs, you will only help yourself in the short-term since, according to REBT, your emotional problem is determined largely by these beliefs and not by any distortions that you may have made at 'A' (see Chapter 10).

In this and the previous chapter I have laid the foundations for how you can modify your thinking and change your behaviour when they serve to largely determine and maintain your emotional problem. In Chapters 4–10, I will build on these foundations to consider the nuts and bolts of doing so.

4

identifying and formulating your problems and goals

CBT recommends adopting a problem-solving approach to your problems and thus it is important that you specify your problems in a way that helps you best to tackle them and to set specific and realistic goals so that you know where you are heading. In this chapter, I will help you to use REBT theory to formulate your problems and goals. When formulating a problem, I will suggest that you select your main unhealthy negation emotion at 'C' and also identify the behavioural 'C's' and thinking 'C's' that go along with this emotional 'C'. Then, I urge you to identify the situations in which you experience the problem and the major theme at 'A'. The 'A' is what you are most disturbed about. When formulating a goal, I will show you that the situations and the theme at 'A' is the same as in your formulated problem. Only your emotion, behaviour and thinking at 'C' will be different and more constructive.

The importance of identifying your problems and goals

You can get the most out of this book if you too develop a problem list and your goals with respect to each problem on the list. Doing so provides a direction for the process and helps prevent you from floundering around, not knowing where you are headed.

Formulating your problems and goals using REBT

Now that you have put your problems and goals into your own words, you are ready to formulate them using insights derived from REBT. In what follows, I will be drawing on the 'Situational ABC' framework that I first described in Chapter 2 and you might find it useful to re-read that chapter before you use the following steps.

Formulate your emotional problems

I suggest that you use the following steps in formulating each of your emotional problems:

['Situations'] – Identify the situations in which you experience your problem.

['A'] – Identify the theme of the problem. Ask yourself what is it about the situations that you specified that is a problem for you. This is likely to be an inference. Consult Table 3.1 for help on this point.

['C' (Emotional)] – Identify the one major unhealthy negative emotion that you experience when you encounter the situations and theme that you specified above.

['C' (Behavioural)] – Identify the dysfunctional behaviour that you demonstrate in these situations.

['C' (Thinking)] – Identify the thinking you engage in once your unhealthy negative emotion has 'kicked in'.

Formulate your goals

I suggest that you use the following steps in formulating each of your goals:

[**Situations**] – Identify the situations in which you experience your problem. This will be the same as you listed in the 'situations' section of your formulated problem above.

['**A**'] – Identify the theme of the problem. Ask yourself what is it about the situations that you specified that is a problem for you. This is likely to be an inference and will be the same as you listed under 'A' in your formulated problem above.

['**C' (Emotional Goal)**] – Identify the healthy alternative to the major unhealthy negative emotion that you experienced when you encountered the situations and theme that you specified above. Note that this emotional goal should be negative because it is about an adversity, but it should also be healthy in the sense that it will enable you to deal effectively with the adversity if it can be changed or to adjust constructively to it if it cannot be changed.

['**C' (Behavioural Goal)**] – Identify the functional alternative to the unconstructive behaviour that you demonstrated.

['**C' (Thinking Goal)**] – Identify the realistic alternative to the highly distorted thinking that you engaged in.

Note that when you formulate goals for your emotional problems, you are changing only your emotional, behavioural and thinking responses to the situations and theme in these situations that you find problematic. This is because in REBT we want you to be prepared to face life's adversities even when you think that an adversity will happen when in fact it doesn't.

Also, note that under the headings of 'emotional goal', 'behavioural goal' and 'thinking goal', I suggest that you use the 'rather than' wording to highlight the difference between your problem response and your goal response. However, if you find doing this cumbersome, then omit the 'rather than' phrases.

In the next chapter I will discuss choosing and working with a target problem and a specific example of that problem.

5

selecting and working with a target problem

CBT works best, at least initially, when you work on one problem at a time. As such selecting the problem you are going to focus on – known as your target problem – needs care. I suggest that when selecting a target problem you choose one (i) with which you are currently preoccupied; (ii) that is easiest to tackle or (iii) that will engender the most hope in you. Once you have selected a target problem, keep your focus on this problem until you have dealt effectively with it. Only change focus if you are preoccupied with another emotional problem and you can't concentrate on the target problem or something far more serious has happened to you which needs urgent attention. Selecting a specific example of your target problem will help you assess your problem in greater detail.

When you select a specific example, choose one that is emotionally laden, typical, vivid and recent, or imminent.

In the previous chapter I suggested that you develop a problem and goal list. I then helped you to formulate each problem and related goal using REBT theory. Having done this, you are ready to tackle your problems one at a time.

Selecting a target problem

You may be thinking, why work on my problems one at a time? Why not work on them all at once or in batches? There are a number of reasons why I suggest that you work on one problem, especially at the beginning of the self-change process:

* **Don't be a tired clown!** Have you ever been to the circus and watched a clown try to keep eight saucers spinning on eight long sticks? All is well at the beginning, but after a while the clown becomes tired and eventually all the plates come crashing to earth. If you try to deal with all your problems at once (or even in smaller batches), you will eventually become exhausted and will end up not helping yourself with any of your problems. So, selecting and dealing with one problem at a time, at least initially, helps you not become a tired clown!

* **Don't be a confused horse – wear blinkers!** If you try to deal with all your problems at once (or even in smaller batches), you will quite soon become quite confused and your mind will wander from one problem to the next and back again. Some racehorses wear blinkers. Why? Because otherwise their attention will wander and they will not be able to do their best in the race. Wearing blinkers helps them to focus. Likewise, selecting and working with one problem at a time will help you to focus and get the best out of REBT.

* **Focusing helps you to learn new skills!** Throughout this book, I am going to teach you and help you

learn new skills. If you implement and practise these skills you will increase the chances that you will help yourself address your emotional problems effectively. Learning any new skill is usually difficult and you will maximize the chances of learning the skills in this book if you focus on one problem at a time without the added distraction of dealing with two or more problems at once.

When you have chosen a problem to work on this is known as your **target problem**. The term 'target problem' can best be thought of as the problem you have targeted to work on first.

Criteria for selecting your target problem

If you are not clear which problem you should select as your target problem, then let me suggest the following criteria that you might find helpful.

Current preoccupation

You may wish to select as your target problem that problem with which you are currently preoccupied. The advantage of this criterion is that you are working on a problem where your focus is naturally. However, this problem may be very difficult to address or may not be suitable to tackle first for other reasons and thus you may not choose to select it as your target problem.

Easiest to tackle

You may wish to select as your target problem that problem for your list that is, in your view, easiest to tackle. On the grounds that nothing succeeds better than success, if you are able to deal with your easiest problem then you may develop the confidence to address a more complex problem. Of course, if you target your easiest problem and do not succeed in addressing it successfully, you may well become discouraged about applying REBT to your problems.

Engenders hope

Finally, you may wish to select as your target problem that problem from your list that if you address effectively will inspire you with hope for the future. Again the danger is that if you do not address it effectively, you may become hopeless.

I suggest that you consider the above criteria and ask yourself which criterion is likely to help you in the long run. Choose the criterion that you resonate with the most and use this to select your target problem.

Working with the target problem all the way through

In the television quiz *Mastermind*, when the quizmaster, John Humphrys, has started asking a question, but is interrupted by the end of round buzzer, he responds: 'I've started, so I'll finish.' This is sound advice when it comes to working on your target problem. So, once you have selected a target problem, it is best if you continue with it rather than 'chopping and changing' and going from one problem to the next without achieving closure on the target problem.

Having made this general point, there are, of course, exceptions to this rule. I will mention two:

1 Remain with the target problem, unless another problem has come to occupy your mental space and you cannot sufficiently 'park' this other problem. In which case change to this problem.

2 Remain with the target problem unless another problem has emerged that is far more serious than the target problem. Again, if this happens change to this problem.

However, if you find that you keep changing from problem to problem despite resolving to sticking with one, then you may need some professional assistance to help you understand the reasons for this continual shifting from problem to problem. Once this issue has been resolved and you can work with your target problem over time then you can resume using this book for self-help purposes.

Selecting a specific example of the target problem

Once you have selected a particular problem to work on from your problem list, it is particularly important that you follow on from this by selecting a specific example of this problem to work on. In Chapter 2 I presented the 'Situational ABC' framework which has been designed to help you to understand your problems in their situational context. I pointed out in that chapter that we experience our problems in specific situations and therefore working with a specific example of your target problem will help you to understand the 'ABC' of your problem as you actually experience it – i.e. in a specific situational context.

Thus, a specific example of your target problem is one where you can provide the following information as I discussed in Chapter 2:

Where you were
When you were there
Who else was present
What happened.

Here are some suggestions about selecting a specific example of your target problem.

Select an *emotionally laden* example of your target problem

It is best if you pick a specific example that is fresh in your mind and one that has emotional resonance for you. If you are likely to feel the disturbed emotion (at 'C') as you focus on the event then so much the better, as experiencing the emotion (at 'C') will enable you to identify the other elements of the 'ABC' model more easily than if you experience no emotion as you focus on the event.

Select a *typical* example of your target problem

A typical example of your target problem is one that occurs frequently. As such you may have many examples to choose from, which is an advantage. However, there is also the danger, if you are not careful, of fusing two or more examples in your mind, with the result that your resultant 'fused' example loses its emotional impact and the information that you are likely to give about 'ABC' factors in your 'fused' example is likely to be theoretical. To guard against this, use the 'where, when, who, what' framework in working with a typical example of your target problem.

Select a *recent* example of your target problem

The advantage of selecting a recent example of your target problem is that, as it is recent, you should be able to recall it without too much difficulty. However, if the example is not very memorable or if some of the problem's main features may not be present, it is best not to use a recent example.

Select a *vivid* example of your target problem

A vivid example of your target problem is one that stands out in your mind. It will therefore probably provide you with emotionally laden information that will enable you to identify more easily the relevant 'ABC' factors. However, because it is vivid it may not be representative of your problem as you normally experience it. Bear this in mind when thinking about selecting a vivid example of your target problem.

Select an *imminent* example of your target problem

An imminent example of your target problem is one that has not actually occurred yet, but that you predict will occur in the foreseeable future. The main advantage of selecting an imminent example of your target problem is that it gives self-help a forward-looking impetus and helps you to choose a relevant homework assignment (see Chapter 8) so that you face up to your predicted adversity and practise the skills that I will teach you later in the book. Using imminent examples of your target problem is particularly useful for anxiety problems and for dealing with procrastination or other forms of avoidance.

The main disadvantage of selecting an imminent example of your target problem is that, as the event has not yet happened, you may not be able to envision with sufficient clarity the specific event that exists only in your mind.

In summary, the very best specific example of your target problem is one that is:

* recent or imminent
* emotionally laden
* vivid *and*
* typical.

The more of these factors you can incorporate in your selected specific example, the better.

The worst specific example you can choose is one that:

* has happened long ago or you think will happen far into the future
* has little present emotional impact on you
* is unclear *and*
* is untypical.

The fewer of these factors you can incorporate in your selected specific example, the better.

In the following chapter I will discuss using the 'Situational ABC' framework to assess a chosen example of a target problem and to set goals for this problem.

using the 'Situational ABC' framework

You are now ready to use the 'Situational ABC' framework to assess your selected specific example of your target problem. Start off by describing the situation in which you disturbed yourself as clearly and concretely as possible. Then, begin with your 'C' which is usually an unhealthy negative emotion, but may be an overt behaviour or an action tendency and use this to identify what you are most disturbed about at 'A'. It is important at this stage that you assume temporarily that your 'A' is true since doing so will help you to identify your irrational beliefs. Then, set emotional, behavioural and thinking goals with respect to the specific example of your target problem. Finally, identify the irrational beliefs (rigid and extreme beliefs) that underpin your disturbed response and the rational beliefs (flexible and non-extreme beliefs) that underpin your goals.

While reading the steps that I discuss in this chapter, I suggest that you refer to the self-help form that I present at the end of the book. You may wish to use this form from now on. However, feel free to modify it or even construct your own form.

Give a brief description of the 'situation'

As I pointed out in Chapter 2, you experience your emotional problems in specific situations even if these situations are in your mind. Your task here is to write down on the form, under the heading 'Situation', a brief, objective description of the 'situation' you were in when you disturbed yourself. As I discussed in Chapters 2 and 5, it is useful to keep in mind the following 'Ws' when describing the situation:

Where you were
When you were there
Who else was present
What happened.

Identify 'C'

After you have described the 'situation', the next step is to focus on the responses that comprised your emotional problem. These are placed at 'C' in the 'Situational ABC' framework. You may be wondering at this point why I am suggesting that you start with 'C' and not with 'A'. In my experience, knowing your disturbed emotion at 'C' helps you to identify 'A' more easily than knowing your 'A' helps you to identify 'C'. However, as the form shows, the steps where you identify 'A' and 'C' are interchangeable, and if you want to identify 'A' before 'C', that's fine.

You will remember from Chapter 2 that there are three types of 'C' that we are interested in: the *emotional*, *behavioural* and *thinking* consequences of your irrational beliefs.

Let me consider these one at a time.

Identify your major unhealthy negative emotion (UNE)

Here are some tips to help you to identify your major UNE.

Look at your formulated problem for your specific unhealthy negative emotion

In Chapter 4 I showed you how to formulate your problems in general terms. So, when you experience one of your formulated problems in a specific situation, it should be easy to identify your specific UNE – it will be substantially the same emotion as the one listed in your formulated problem.

Common unhealthy negative emotions

There are times, however, when you may disturb yourself about other adversities that do not appear in your formulated problems. In such circumstances, you need to start from the beginning in identifying the main unhealthy negative emotion that you experienced in this situation. As before, you need to be specific in identifying your UNE, since doing so will help you to identify the other elements in the 'Situational ABC' framework. The following list outlines the main UNEs for which people seek help: anxiety, depression, guilt, shame, hurt, unhealthy anger, unhealthy jealousy and unhealthy envy.

Try to identify your major UNE from the above list and avoid vague statements of emotion such as 'I felt bad' or 'I felt upset'. Also avoid using terms that are really adversities at 'A' such as 'I felt rejected' and 'I felt criticized'.

What if you have more than one UNE in the situation?

You can experience more than one UNE in any given situation. Thus, imagine that your boss has asked you to do a presentation at short notice. You may feel anxious and unhealthily angry about this. You may feel anxious about giving a poor presentation and unhealthily angry with your boss for putting you on the spot at short notice.

In such situations, choose the UNE that represents your biggest problem and work with that one first. However, at this point, what is more important is once you have chosen one UNE that you stick with this problem until you have dealt with it before switching to the other problem.

The difference between healthy and unhealthy negative emotions

You may be uncertain whether the negative emotion that you experienced in your selected example was unhealthy or healthy. If you misunderstand the difference between the two, you may try to change a healthy negative emotion.

There are three major ways of distinguishing between unhealthy and healthy negative emotions:

1 UNEs stem from irrational beliefs, while HNEs stem from rational beliefs.
2 UNEs are associated with behaviours that are dysfunctional, while HNEs are associated with behaviours that are functional.
3 UNEs are associated with thinking that is highly unrealistic and skewed to the negative, while HNEs are associated with thinking that is realistic and balanced.

Once you have identified your major UNE, write it on the form (at the end of the book) next to 'C (emotional consequence)'.

Identify your dysfunctional behaviour

As I pointed out above, when you experience an unhealthy negative emotion, your associated behaviour is likely to be dysfunctional and as such it will make your emotional problem worse. As I pointed out in Chapter 2, there are two types of behaviour that you need to identify at 'C':

1 actual behaviours that are observable and
2 action tendencies where you 'feel like' acting in a certain way, but do not.

There are certain forms of behaviour that are frequently associated with particular unhealthy negative emotions. I provided a representative list in Table 1.2, but of course your job is to detail how you acted in the situation or what you 'felt like' doing, but did not. Write this on the form next to 'C (behavioural consequence)'.

Identify your subsequent distorted thinking

When you feel an unhealthy negative emotion and act in a dysfunctional way at 'C', you also tend to think in ways that are highly distorted and exaggerated. I call this thinking 'subsequent distorted thinking' because it stems from irrational beliefs and because it is distorted in nature. There are certain forms of thinking that are frequently associated with particular unhealthy negative emotions. I provide a representative list in Table 6.1, but again your job is to identify your subsequent thinking in the example situation that you are assessing and write it on the form next to 'C (thinking consequence)'.

Table 6.1 Unhealthy negative emotions and illustrative subsequent distorted thinking.

Unhealthy negative emotion	Subsequent distorted thinking
Anxiety	Overestimating the negative consequences of the threat if it occurs
Depression	Hopelessness Helplessness
Guilt	Assigning too much responsibility to yourself and too little to others
Shame	Overestimating the negativity of others' reactions to yourself and the extent of these reactions
Hurt	Thinking that the other has to put things right of their own accord
Unhealthy anger	Thinking that the other has malicious intent Thoughts of exacting revenge
Unhealthy jealousy	Tending to see threats to your relationship in the absence of evidence
Unhealthy envy	Tending to denigrate the value of the desired possession

You will recall that 'A' stands for 'adversity'. It represents what you were most disturbed about in the situation that provided the context for your emotional problem. While I suggested earlier that it might be useful to identify 'C' before 'A', these steps are, in fact, interchangeable and, if you prefer, you should identify 'A' before 'C'.

Consult your formulated problem

In Chapter 4 I discussed how to identify your problems and goals. You will recall that I showed you how to formulate your problem using REBT theory as a guide. If you take your formulated problem together with the specific example of this problem which you are assessing, then it may well be that the 'A' in your specific example will be a specific representation of the more general 'A' in your formulated problem. Ask yourself a relevant question such as: Is what I am most disturbed about in this specific example the same as what I am disturbed about in my formulated problem?

Identifying the specific example of the theme

When you are endeavouring to identify your 'A', you might find it helpful to consult Table 1.1. This table lists the common inferential themes associated with the eight major unhealthy negative emotions. What you do is this:

* Use your major UNE at 'C' to identify your general theme (e.g. threat in anxiety) at 'A'.
* Ask yourself the following question (the content will vary according to the general theme at 'A' and your major UNE at 'C'): What did I find most threatening in this situation?
* The answer is probably your specific 'A' in your chosen example.

Using the 'magic question'

When you use the 'magic question' technique to identify your 'A', you do the following:

* Focus on the 'situation' that you have described.
* Ask yourself what one thing would get rid of or significantly diminish the unhealthy negative emotion that you felt at 'C'.
* The opposite to this is your 'A'.

Assume temporarily that 'A' is true

Once you have identified your adversity at 'A', you may discover that it represents a clear distortion of reality. If this is the case, you may be tempted to question 'A'. Resist this temptation. Rather, at this stage you should assume temporarily that 'A' is correct.

Later, you will have an opportunity to check whether your 'A' is likely to have been true (see Chapter 10).

Set emotional, behavioural and thinking goals

At some point in working with your specific example of your target problem, it is important to set goals with respect to the example. Here, realize that you will only be changing your responses to your adversity at 'A' and not the adversity itself. The whole point of what you are doing here is to help you to respond healthily to adversities. When you do so, you will be in a better frame of mind to attempt to change or realistically reinterpret 'A' than if you tried to do these things when you were disturbed about 'A'.

Set your emotional goal

When you set emotional goals, bear in mind that you will be selecting a healthy negative emotion. The emotion will be negative because your adversity is negative, but it will be healthy.

In Chapter 2 I discussed the healthy alternatives to unhealthy negative emotions and these are presented below. However, as I have previously mentioned, it is important that you use your own term for the relevant healthy emotion rather than the one listed: concern (rather than anxiety), sadness (rather than depression), remorse (rather than guilt), disappointment (rather than shame), sorrow (rather than hurt), healthy anger (rather than unhealthy anger), healthy jealousy (rather than unhealthy jealousy), healthy envy (rather than unhealthy envy).

Set your behavioural goal

When you experience a healthy negative emotion, your associated behaviour is likely to be functional and as such it will help you to overcome your emotional problem. Your functional behavioural goal will be the opposite of your dysfunctional behaviour. As with dysfunctional behaviour, functional behaviour can be overt or an action tendency.

There are certain forms of behaviour that are frequently associated with particular healthy negative emotions. I provided a representative list in Table 1.2, but your job is to identify the healthy alternatives to your unhealthy behaviour. When you have done so, write this on the form next to 'C (behavioural goal)'.

Set your thinking goal

When you feel a healthy negative emotion and act in a functional way at 'C', you also tend to think in ways that are realistic and balanced in nature. I call this thinking 'subsequent realistic thinking' because it stems from rational beliefs and because it is realistic in nature. This thinking represents your thinking goal in the situation being assessed and should thus be placed under 'C (thinking goal)' on the form. It is a direct realistic and balanced alternative to the subsequent distorted thinking that you wrote down under 'C (thinking consequence)'. There are certain forms of thinking that are frequently associated with particular healthy negative emotions. I provide a representative list in Table 6.2.

Table 6.2 Healthy negative emotions and illustrative subsequent realistic and balanced thinking.

Healthy negative emotion	Subsequent realistic and balanced thinking
Concern (rather than anxiety)	Being realistic about the negative consequences of the threat if it occurs
Sadness (rather than depression)	Able to see good things happening in the future as well as bad Able to see yourself taking steps to help yourself
Remorse (rather than guilt)	Assigning the appropriate amount of responsibility to yourself and to others
Disappointment (rather than shame)	Being realistic concerning the negativity of others' reactions to you and the extent of these reactions
Sorrow (rather than hurt)	Thinking that you can sort the issue out with the other rather than waiting for that person to put things right of their own accord
Healthy anger (rather than problematic anger)	Thinking that the other may have malicious intent but not necessarily so Thoughts of communicating your feelings to the other and how to do so
Healthy jealousy (rather than problematic jealousy)	Tending to see threats to your relationship only in the presence of evidence
Healthy envy (rather than problematic envy)	Tending to appreciate rather than denigrate the value of the desired possession

Identify your irrational beliefs (iBs)

You have now identified the 'A' and 'C' components of the specific example of your target problem and relevant goals. The next step is to identify your irrational beliefs at 'B' that accounted for your responses at 'C' to the adversity at 'A'. You will recall from Chapter 2 that there are four irrational beliefs: one rigid belief and three extreme beliefs (see Table 6.3).

Table 6.3 Irrational beliefs.

Rigid belief	'I / You / Life must...'
	↓
Extreme awfulizing belief	'It's awful that...'
Extreme discomfort intolerance belief	'I can't bear it...'
Extreme depreciation belief (self, other, life)	'I / You / Life is no good...'

In order to identify your irrational beliefs I suggest that you do the following:
* Take your 'A'.
* Identify the rigid belief that you held about 'A'.
* Identify the main extreme belief that you held about 'A'.
* Put all this information together.

(This is your composite irrational belief which you write down under the heading 'iB' – irrational belief – on the form at the end of the book)

Identify the alternative rational beliefs (rBs)

The final step is for you to identify the rational beliefs that are the healthy alternatives to your already identified irrational beliefs. These beliefs will enable you to achieve your emotional, behavioural and thinking goals that you have listed on the right-hand side of the form. As we saw in Chapter 2, there are four irrational beliefs: one flexible belief and three non-extreme beliefs (see Table 6.4).

Table 6.4 Rational beliefs.

Flexible belief	*'It would be preferable if I / You Life…, but it is not necessary…'*
	↓
Non-extreme non-awfulizing belief	*'It's bad, but not terrible that…'*
Non-extreme discomfort tolerance belief	*'It's hard, but I can bear it and it is worth it to me to do so…'*
Non-extreme acceptance belief (self, other, life)	*'I / You / Life is complex and too complex to be given a single rating…'*

In order to identify your alternative rational belief, you provide the flexible alternative to your rigid belief and the non-extreme alternative to your major extreme belief and then combine them. Then, you write this down on the 'Situational ABC' form (at the end of the book) under the heading 'rB (rational belief)'.

7

focusing on and questioning your beliefs

You are now ready to question your rational and irrational beliefs, which is the heart of the change process in REBT. While there are a number of ways in which you can do this, perhaps the best way is to question them both at the same time to help you see more clearly the differences between them. Thus, question your rigid and flexible beliefs separately from your extreme and non-extreme beliefs. I suggest that you get into the habit of always questioning your rigid and flexible beliefs and at least your most relevant extreme and non-extreme beliefs. When questioning your beliefs, ask about their validity (true or false), logical status (sensible or nonsensical) and pragmatic value (constructive or unconstructive). Continue the questioning process until you can acknowledge that your irrational beliefs are irrational (i.e. false, illogical and unconstructive) and your rational beliefs are rational (i.e. true, logical, and constructive).

In the previous chapter I showed you how to assess a specific example of your target problem and set appropriate emotional, behavioural and thinking goals. These goals are best achieved when you hold rational rather than irrational beliefs about the adversity in question at 'A'.

I showed you in the previous chapter how to identify your irrational beliefs and their rational alternatives. In this chapter I will discuss and illustrate how you can stand back and evaluate both of these beliefs so that you can commit yourself to strengthening your rational beliefs and weakening your irrational beliefs (see Chapter 8).

I am going to deal with rigid and flexible beliefs separately from extreme and non-extreme beliefs and when I consider the latter I will do so one at a time.

Questioning your beliefs: general issues

When you question your beliefs, you need to keep the following general issues in mind:

1 The purpose of questioning your beliefs is to help you decide which beliefs you want to operate on in future. In doing so, you need to ask yourself a number of questions:
   * which belief is true and which is false and specify the reasons why
   * which belief is sensible and which is illogical and the reasons why
   * which belief has the healthiest consequences for you and which has the unhealthiest consequences and why.
2 You need to question both your irrational beliefs and your rational beliefs. If you only question your irrational beliefs you may understand that they are false, illogical and unhealthy, but you may not automatically see that your alternative rational beliefs are true, logical and healthy. You may only see this if you question your rational beliefs in the same way as you questioned your irrational beliefs.

3 You can question your beliefs in a number of orders. Thus, you may question all your relevant irrational beliefs first before you question your alternative rational beliefs. In this book I advocate you questioning your rigid and flexible beliefs together and then your relevant extreme and non-extreme beliefs together. However, in doing so, I am not saying that this is the only order that you can employ to question your irrational and rational beliefs. If you find another order more useful, by all means employ it.

4 At the very least, I suggest that you question your rigid and flexible beliefs. If you do question your extreme and non-extreme beliefs, you don't need to question all three. Preferably, you should question the main extreme belief that stems from your rigid belief and that best accounts for your disturbed emotion at 'C' and its non-extreme belief alternative.

Questioning your rigid and flexible beliefs

It is important to remember that at this point you are dealing with the specific rigid belief that you identified in Chapter 6 and its specific flexible alternative. I will deal with more general core beliefs in Chapter 11.

Here are the steps that I suggest you take while questioning your rigid and flexible beliefs.

1 Write down your rigid and flexible beliefs side by side on a piece of paper.

2 Ask yourself the following question: Which of these two beliefs is true and which is false? Give reasons for your answer. In Table 7.1 I provide suggestions to help you do this.

3 Ask yourself the following question: Which of these two beliefs is logical or sensible and which is illogical? Give reasons for your answer. In Table 7.1 I provide suggestions to help you do this.

4 Ask yourself the following question: Which of these two beliefs is most healthy for me and which is least healthy? Give reasons for your answer. In Table 7.1 I provide suggestions to help you do this.

5 On the basis of the above, you should now be in a position to commit yourself to strengthening your conviction in your flexible belief and to weakening your conviction in your rigid belief. I will deal with this issue more fully in the next chapter. To put this commitment into practice, I suggest the first step is for you to write down the arguments that you find most persuasive which show why your rigid belief is irrational and why your flexible belief is rational.

Table 7.1 Reasons why rigid beliefs are false and illogical and have largely unhealthy consequences and why flexible beliefs are true and logical and have largely healthy consequences.

Rigid belief	Flexible belief
A rigid belief is false	**A flexible belief is true**
For such a demand to be true the demanded conditions would already have to exist when they do not. Or as soon as you make a demand then these demanded conditions would have to come into existence. Both positions are clearly false or inconsistent with reality.	A flexible belief is true because its two component parts are true. You can prove that you have a particular desire and can provide reasons why you want what you want. You can also prove that you do not have to get what you desire.
A rigid belief is illogical	**A flexible belief is logical**
A rigid belief is based on the same desire as a flexible but is transformed as follows:	A flexible belief is logical since both parts are not rigid and thus the second component logically follows from the first. Thus, consider the following flexible belief:

Rigid belief	Flexible belief
'I prefer that x happens (or does not happen) and therefore this absolutely must (or must not) happen.'	*'I prefer that x happens (or does not happen)...but this does not mean that it must (or must not) happen.'*
The first ('I prefer that x happens (or does not happen...)') is not rigid, but the second ('...and therefore this must (or must not) happen') is rigid. As such, a rigid belief is illogical since one cannot logically derive something rigid from something that is not rigid.	The first component ('I prefer that x happens (or does not happen...)') is not rigid and the second ('...but this does not mean that it must (or must not) happen') is also non-rigid. Thus, a flexible belief is logical because it comprises two non-rigid parts connected together logically.
A rigid belief has largely unhealthy consequences	**A flexible belief has largely healthy consequences**
A rigid belief has largely unhealthy consequences because it tends to lead to unhealthy negative emotions, unconstructive behaviour and highly distorted and biased subsequent thinking when the person is facing an adversity.	A flexible belief has largely healthy consequences because it tends to lead to healthy negative emotions, constructive behaviour, and realistic and balanced subsequent thinking when the person is facing an adversity.

I am now going to show you how to question your extreme beliefs and their non-extreme alternatives. As I do so, remember that I said that you do not have to question all three extreme and non-extreme beliefs. Rather, I suggested that you focus on the following:

* the one major extreme belief that, along with your rigid belief, in your view accounted for your disturbed feelings at 'C' *and*
* its non-extreme alternative.

Questioning your awfulizing and non-awfulizing beliefs

If you have chosen your awfulizing and non-awfulizing beliefs as the most relevant extreme and non-extreme beliefs to question, it is important to remember that you are dealing with the specific beliefs that you identified in Chapter 6. I will deal with more general core beliefs in Chapter 11.

Here are the steps that I suggest you take while questioning your awfulizing and non-awfulizing beliefs.

1 Write down your awfulizing and non-awfulizing beliefs side by side on a piece of paper.
2 Ask yourself the following question: Which of these two beliefs is true and which is false? Give reasons for your answer. In Table 7.2, I provide suggestions to help you do this.
3 Ask yourself the following question: Which of these two beliefs is logical or sensible and which is illogical? Give reasons for your answer. In Table 7.2 I provide suggestions to help you do this.
4 Ask yourself the following question: Which of these two beliefs is most healthy for me and which is least healthy? Give reasons for your answer. In Table 7.2 I provide suggestions to help you do this.
5 On the basis of the above, you should now be in a position to commit yourself to strengthening your conviction in your non-awfulizing belief and to weakening your conviction in your awfulizing belief. I will deal with this issue more fully in the next chapter. To put this commitment into practice, I suggest the first step is for you to write down the arguments that most persuasively show why your awfulizing belief is irrational and why your non-awfulizing belief is rational.

Table 7.2 Reasons why awfulizing beliefs are false and illogical and have largely unhealthy consequences and why non-awfulizing beliefs are true and logical and have largely healthy consequences.

Awfulizing belief	Non-awfulizing belief
An awfulizing belief is false	**A non-awfulizing belief is true**
When you hold an awfulizing belief about your 'A', this belief is based on the following ideas: i) Nothing could be worse. ii) The event in question is worse than 100 per cent bad. iii) No good could possibly come from this bad event. All three ideas are patently false and thus your awfulizing belief is false.	When you hold a non-awfulizing belief about your 'A', this belief is based on the following ideas: i) Things could always be worse. ii) The event in question is less than 100 per cent bad. iii) Good could come from this bad event. All three ideas are clearly true and thus your non-awfulizing belief is true.
An awfulizing belief is illogical	**A non-awfulizing belief is logical**
An awfulizing belief is based on the same evaluation of badness as a non-awfulizing belief, but is transformed as follows:	A non-awfulizing belief is logical since both parts are non-rigid and thus the second component logically follows from the first. Thus, consider the following non-awfulizing belief:
'It is bad if x happens (or does not happen)... and therefore it is awful if it does happen (or does not happen).'	*'It is bad if x happens (or does not happen)... but it is not awful if x happens (or does not happen).'*
The first component ('It is bad if x happens (or does not happen...)') is non-extreme, but the second ('...and therefore it is awful if it	The first component ('It is bad if x happens (or does not happen...)') is non-extreme and the second ('...but it is not awful if it does (or does not

(Contd)

Awfulizing belief	Non-awfulizing belief
does (or does not) happen)') is extreme. As such, an awfulizing belief is illogical since one cannot logically derive something extreme from something that is non-extreme.	happen') is also non-extreme. Thus, a non-awfulizing belief is logical because it comprises two non-extreme parts connected together logically.
An awfulizing belief has largely unhealthy consequences	**A non-awfulizing belief has largely healthy consequences**
An awfulizing belief has largely unhealthy consequences because it tends to lead to unhealthy negative emotions, unconstructive behaviour and highly distorted and biased subsequent thinking when the person is facing an adversity.	A non-awfulizing belief has largely healthy consequences because it tends to lead to healthy negative emotions, constructive behaviour and realistic and balanced subsequent thinking when the person is facing an adversity.

Questioning your discomfort intolerance and discomfort tolerance beliefs

If you have chosen your discomfort intolerance and discomfort tolerance beliefs as the most relevant extreme and non-extreme beliefs to question, it is important to remember that you are dealing with the specific beliefs that you identified in Chapter 6. I will deal with more general core beliefs in Chapter 11.

Here are the steps that I suggest you take while questioning your discomfort intolerance and discomfort tolerance beliefs.

1 Write down your discomfort intolerance and discomfort tolerance beliefs side by side on a piece of paper.

2 Ask yourself the following question: Which of these two beliefs is true and which is false? Give reasons for your answer. In Table 7.3, I provide suggestions to help you do this.

3 Ask yourself the following question: Which of these two beliefs is logical or sensible and which is illogical? Give reasons for your answer. In Table 7.3, I provide suggestions to help you do this.

4 Ask yourself the following question: Which of these two beliefs is most healthy for me and which is least healthy? Give reasons for your answer. In Table 7.3, I provide suggestions to help you do this.

5 On the basis of the above, you should now be in a position to commit yourself to strengthening your conviction in your discomfort tolerance belief and to weakening your conviction in your discomfort intolerance belief. I will deal with this issue more fully in the next chapter. To put this commitment into practice, I suggest the first step is for you to write down the arguments that you find most persuasive which show why your discomfort intolerance belief is irrational and why your discomfort tolerance belief is rational.

Table 7.3 Reasons why discomfort intolerance beliefs are false and illogical and have largely unhealthy consequences and why discomfort tolerance beliefs are true and logical and have largely healthy consequences.

Discomfort intolerance belief	Discomfort tolerance belief
A discomfort intolerance belief is false	**A discomfort tolerance belief is true**
When you hold a discomfort intolerance belief about your	When you hold a discomfort tolerance belief about your

(Contd)

Discomfort intolerance belief	Discomfort tolerance belief

'A', this belief is based on the following ideas which are all false:

i) I will die or disintegrate if the discomfort continues to exist.
ii) I will lose the capacity to experience happiness if the discomfort continues to exist.
iii) Even if I could tolerate it, the discomfort is not worth tolerating.

All three ideas are patently false and thus your discomfort intolerance belief is false.

A discomfort intolerance belief is illogical

A discomfort intolerance belief is based on the same sense of struggle as a discomfort tolerance belief, but is transformed as follows:

'It would be difficult for me to tolerate it if x happens (or does not happen)... and therefore it would be intolerable.'

'A', this belief is based on the following ideas which are all true:

i) I will struggle if the discomfort continues to exist, but I will neither die nor disintegrate.
ii) I will not lose the capacity to experience happiness if the discomfort continues to exist, although this capacity will be temporarily diminished.
iii) The discomfort is worth tolerating.

All three ideas are patently true and thus your discomfort tolerance belief is true.

A discomfort tolerance belief is logical

A discomfort tolerance belief is logical since both parts are non-extreme and thus the second component logically follows from the first. Thus, consider the following discomfort tolerance belief:

'It would be difficult for me to tolerate it if x happens (or does not happen)...but it would not be intolerable (and it would be worth tolerating).'

Discomfort intolerance belief	Discomfort tolerance belief
The first component ('It would be difficult for me to tolerate it if *x* happens (or does not happen…)') is non-extreme, but the second ('…and therefore it would be intolerable') is extreme. As such, a discomfort intolerance belief is illogical since one cannot logically derive something extreme from something that is non-extreme.	The first component ('It would be difficult for me to tolerate it if *x* happens (or does not happen…)') is non-extreme and the second ('…but it would not be intolerable (and it would be worth tolerating)') is also non-extreme. Thus, a discomfort tolerance belief is logical because it comprises two non-extreme parts connected together logically.

A discomfort intolerance belief has largely unhealthy consequences

A discomfort intolerance belief has largely unhealthy consequences because it tends to lead to unhealthy negative emotions, unconstructive behaviour, and highly distorted and biased subsequent thinking when the person is facing an adversity.

A discomfort tolerance belief has largely healthy consequences

A discomfort tolerance belief has largely healthy consequences because it tends to lead to healthy negative emotions, constructive behaviour, and realistic and balanced subsequent thinking when the person is facing an adversity.

Questioning your depreciation and acceptance beliefs

If you have chosen your depreciation and acceptance beliefs as the most relevant extreme and non-extreme beliefs to question, it is important to remember that you are dealing with the specific beliefs that you identified in Chapter 6. I will deal with more general core beliefs in Chapter 11.

Here are the steps that I suggest you take while questioning your depreciation and acceptance beliefs.

1 Write down your depreciation and acceptance beliefs side by side on a piece of paper.

2 Ask yourself the following question: Which of these two beliefs is true and which is false? Give reasons for your answer. In Table 7.4 I provide suggestions to help you do this.

3 Ask yourself the following question: Which of these two beliefs is logical or sensible and which is illogical? Give reasons for your answer. In Table 7.4 I provide suggestions to help you do this.

4 Ask yourself the following question: Which of these two beliefs is most healthy for me and which is least healthy? Give reasons for your answer. In Table 7.4, I provide suggestions to help you do this.

5 On the basis of the above, you should now be in a position to commit yourself to strengthening your conviction in your acceptance belief and to weakening your conviction in your depreciation belief. I will deal with this issue more fully in the next chapter. To put this commitment into practice, I suggest the first step is for you to write down the arguments that you find most persuasive which show why your depreciation belief is irrational and why your acceptance belief is rational.

Table 7.4 Reasons why depreciation beliefs are false and illogical and have largely unhealthy consequences and why acceptance beliefs are true and logical and have largely healthy consequences.

Depreciation belief	Acceptance belief
A depreciation belief is false	**An acceptance belief is true**
When you hold a depreciation belief in the face of your 'A', this belief is based on the following ideas which are both false:	When you hold an acceptance belief in the face of your 'A', this belief is based on the following ideas which are both true:
i) A person (self or other) or life can legitimately be given a single global rating that defines their or its essence and the worth of a person or of life is dependent upon conditions that change (e.g. my worth goes up when I do well and goes down when I don't do well).	i) A person (self or other) or life cannot legitimately be given a single global rating that defines their or its essence and their or its worth, as far as they or it have it, is not dependent upon conditions that change (e.g. my worth stays the same whether or not I do well).
ii) A person or life can be rated on the basis of one of his or her or its aspects.	ii) Discrete aspects of a person, and life, can be legitimately rated, but a person or life cannot be legitimately rated on the basis of these discrete aspects.
Both of these ideas are patently false and thus your depreciation belief is false.	Both of these ideas are patently true and thus your depreciation belief is true.

(Contd)

Depreciation belief	Acceptance belief
A depreciation belief is illogical	**An acceptance belief is logical**
A depreciation belief is based on the idea that the whole of a person or of life can logically be defined by one of their or its parts. Thus:	An acceptance belief is based on the idea that the whole of a person or of life cannot be defined by one or more of their or its parts. Thus:
'X is bad... and therefore I am bad.'	*'X is bad, but this does not mean that I am bad; I am a fallible human being even though x happened.'*
This is known as the part–whole error, which is illogical.	Here the part–whole illogical error is avoided. Rather it is held that the whole incorporates the part which is logical.
A depreciation belief has largely unhealthy consequences	**An acceptance belief has largely healthy consequences**
A depreciation belief has largely unhealthy consequences because it tends to lead to unhealthy negative emotions, unconstructive behaviour, and highly distorted and biased subsequent thinking when the person is facing an adversity.	An acceptance belief has largely healthy consequences because it tends to lead to healthy negative emotions, constructive behaviour, and realistic and balanced subsequent thinking when the person is facing an adversity.

In the next chapter I will discuss a number of methods that you can use to begin to strengthen your conviction in your rational beliefs and to weaken your conviction in your irrational beliefs.

8

strengthening your conviction in your rational beliefs

In order to strengthen your conviction in your newly developed rational beliefs you need to use more powerful and persuasive methods and this is the subject of this chapter. I will describe three methods to help you to do this. If you repeatedly use these techniques, your conviction in your rational beliefs will increase, but only if you use them with spirit and energy. I will make the point that perhaps the most powerful way of strengthening your conviction in your rational beliefs is to act in ways that are consistent with them. When you do so, it is important that you remember that emotional change will initially lag behind behavioural change and thinking change, but will catch up if you persist in acting in ways that are in line with your rational beliefs.

In this chapter I present a series of techniques designed to help you give more conviction and credence to your rational beliefs and to reduce your conviction in, and reliance on, your irrational beliefs. This is necessary because simply understanding intellectually that your rational beliefs are true, logical and helpful is not enough to effect change. This type of understanding is known as **intellectual insight**.

Although intellectual insight is required to help you change particular rational beliefs, intellectual insight alone is not enough. The kind of insight you will need to promote change is known by REBT therapists as **emotional insight**. This is when your conviction in your rational beliefs leads to healthy emotions, functional (as opposed to dysfunctional) behaviour and, subsequently, realistic and balanced thinking.

In the next sections you will find techniques to help you believe what you understand intellectually. My aim is to illustrate, rather than to be comprehensive in my coverage of these techniques.

The attack–response method

You can strengthen your conviction in a rational belief by responding persuasively to any attacks on such a belief, and the attack–response method is based on this idea.

Instructions on how to use the attack–response method

Write down on a sheet of paper one of your rational beliefs (e.g. 'I would like to be creative, but I don't have to be. If I'm not creative, I am fallible, not stupid').

* On a percentage scale assess your present level of conviction in this belief, with 0 per cent = no conviction and 100 per cent = total conviction (i.e. 'I believe this in my gut and it strongly influences my feelings and my behaviour'). Under your belief write down this rating.
* Think of ways in which this rational belief could be

attacked and write these down. Such an attack may be, for instance, a doubt, reservation or objection to this rational belief. The attack should also include an explicit irrational belief – for example:

- *demand* – where you demand that you must get what you want or must not get what you don't want
- *awfulizing belief* – in which you evaluate not getting what you demand as being the end of the world
- *discomfort intolerance belief* – reflecting the idea that you can't bear the adversity that you are facing
- *depreciation belief* – in which, for instance, you believe that any failure to fulfil your desire proves that you are worthless.

* Make this attack as genuine as you can. The more it reflects what you believe, the better.
* Respond to this attack as fully, persuasively and wholeheartedly as possible. It is vital that you respond to each part of the attack. In particular, do all you can to respond to irrational belief statements and to distorted or unrealistic inferences expressed in the form of a doubt, reservation or objection to the rational belief. Do this as persuasively as you can and note down your response.
* Continue until you have responded to each one of your attacks and until you are unable to come up with any more. Ensure throughout that you maintain your focus on the rational belief that you are aiming to reinforce.

This is not an easy exercise to do, and you may find it helpful to make the initial attacks fairly gentle to start with. After that, as your responses to the attacks improve, you can start to make the attacks more powerful and gradually increase the strength of your attacks. As you make an attack, try to do so in a way that convinces you of its reality. Then, in responding to the attack, do your best to destroy the attack and to reinforce your conviction in your rational belief.

Remember that the aim of this exercise is to strengthen your conviction in your rational belief, so you should only regard the exercise as finished when you have responded to all of your attacks.

When you have responded to all the attacks, revise your ratings of your level of conviction in your rational belief using the 0–100 per cent scale as previously. If you have replied persuasively to your attacks, this rating will have improved markedly.

There are several variations on the attack–response method. For instance, try recording the dialogue on a DVR (digital voice recorder), in which case you should ensure that your response is more forceful in language and tone than your attack.

Rational-emotive imagery

Rational-emotive imagery (REI) is a method of using imagery which is intended to help you practise changing a *specific* irrational belief to its healthy alternative while you focus your mind on what you are most disturbed about in the *particular* situation in which you felt disturbed. You can only use REI while imagining specific situations, and therefore you are advised to use it only to strengthen your conviction in *particular* rational beliefs.

REI hinges on the fact that imagery can be used to help you surmount your problems or, although unintentionally, to practise thinking unhealthily as you imagine a large number of negative situations about which you disturb yourself. In the case of such negative imagery, when you imagine a negative event and disturb yourself about it, you are likely to do so by contemplating the event in your mind's eye and unwittingly rehearsing irrational beliefs about the event. Thus, you may literally practise disturbing yourself and simultaneously strengthen your conviction in your irrational beliefs.

You can fortunately also use your imagination constructively. While imagining, for example, the same negative event, you can practise changing your unhealthy negative emotions to their healthy equivalents by transforming your particular irrational beliefs into particular rational beliefs.

Instructions on how to use REI

* Think of a situation in which you disturbed yourself and identify the aspect of the situation that most disturbed you (e.g. imagine you are about to start work on your dissertation, but are aware that you are not in a very creative frame of mind).
* Close your eyes and imagine the situation as vividly as you can and focus on the worst aspect of the situation – the *adversity* at 'A' (the activating event).
* Let yourself really experience the unhealthy negative emotion that you felt at the time while still concentrating intently on the 'A'. Make sure that your unhealthy negative emotion is *one* of the following: anxiety, depression, shame, guilt, hurt, unhealthy anger, unhealthy jealousy, unhealthy envy.
* Genuinely experience this disturbed emotion for a short while (a few seconds) and then turn your emotional response to a healthy negative emotion, while simultaneously concentrating your mind on the adversity at 'A'. Do not change the intensity of the emotion, only the emotion. Therefore, if your original unhealthy negative emotion was anxiety, change it to concern; change your depression to sadness, shame to disappointment, guilt to remorse, hurt to sorrow, unhealthy anger to healthy anger, unhealthy jealousy to healthy jealousy and unhealthy envy to healthy envy. Thus you change the unhealthy negative emotion into its healthy equivalent, while ensuring that the level of intensity of the new emotion is as strong as the old emotion. Keep experiencing this new emotion for about five minutes, all the time focusing on the adversity at 'A'. If you return to the old, unhealthy negative emotion, bring back the new healthy negative emotion.

* After five minutes, ask yourself how you changed your emotion.
* Ensure that you changed your emotional response by changing your specific irrational belief to its healthy equivalent. If you did not do so (if, for instance, you changed your emotion by changing the 'A' to make it less negative or neutral or by holding an indifference belief about the 'A'), redo the exercise and keep doing so until you have changed your emotion only by changing your specific unhealthy belief to its healthy equivalent.
* Practise REI several times a day, aiming for 30 minutes a day. You could practise it more often and for longer when you are about to face a negative situation about which you are likely to disturb yourself.

Rehearse your rational beliefs while acting and thinking in ways that are consistent with these beliefs

Probably the most powerful method of reinforcing your rational belief is to rehearse it while you face the relevant adversity at 'A' and while you act and think in ways that chime with this rational belief. When your behaviour and thinking are working together and you keep them working together, you make the most of your chances of strengthening your conviction in your rational belief. You also need to refrain from acting and thinking in ways that follow your old irrational belief. It will be difficult for you to prevent yourself from doing so because you are used to acting and thinking in the old unreconstructed ways when your irrational belief is activated. Yet if you monitor your belief, behaviour and subsequent thinking, and respond constructively when you notice unhealthy instances of them, you will obtain valuable experience at strengthening your conviction in your rational belief.

As you work to reinforce your conviction in your rational beliefs, remember the following:

* You may have been using safety-seeking strategies to help you avoid facing adversities or to give you a feeling of comfort and security if you have to face these adversities. If you carry on employing these strategies while trying to change your irrational beliefs you will not change these beliefs. Identify how you use these strategies (which are largely behavioural and thinking-based in nature and can often be subtle and difficult to detect) and confront and dispute the irrational beliefs on which they are frequently based so that you can face the adversities fairly and squarely as you rehearse your developing rational beliefs.

* You will only experience emotional change (from negative and unhealthy to negative and healthy) after regular integrated practice in which you rehearse your rational belief and act and think in ways consistent with these beliefs. Changes in your emotions tend to lag behind behavioural change and thinking change. If you understand this, then you will keep on working to change your belief, behaviour and subsequent thinking and you will not be discouraged when your feelings take longer to change.

* If you wish to strengthen your conviction in your rational beliefs, you need to expose yourself to events that will challenge you, but which will not overwhelm you at that time. To make the most of such exposure, you must do it regularly while rehearsing your target rational belief and thinking realistically. As you progress, keep stretching yourself until you can face more and more challenging events.

In the next chapter I will offer suggestions on how to deal with the highly distorted negative thinking consequences of irrational beliefs.

responding to highly distorted thoughts at 'C'

In this chapter, I will consider the thinking consequences of irrational beliefs. These are highly distorted and skewed to the negative and more distorted than the inferences that you have made at 'A' since they have been processed by irrational beliefs while the latter have not. I will also outline the common thinking errors that stem from irrational beliefs and the realistic and balanced thinking alternatives to these thinking errors that, in turn, stem from rational beliefs. I will then discuss three ways of responding constructively to the thinking consequences of irrational beliefs. First, you can use them to identify and respond to underlying irrational beliefs. Second, you can consider the evidence for and against the thinking consequences of irrational beliefs and their realistic and balanced alternatives. Finally, you can acknowledge the existences of these thoughts, but choose not to engage with them.

Previously, I have shown you how to change:

a your unhealthy negative emotions to their healthy equivalents

b your unconstructive behaviours to their constructive equivalents.

In this chapter, I will show you how to recognize the thinking consequences of your irrational beliefs and how to respond to them.

How to recognize the thinking consequences of irrational beliefs

The thinking consequences of irrational beliefs (hereafter in this chapter referred to as TCs) are generally forms of thinking that you engage in once 'under the influence', so to speak, of your irrational beliefs. Here are some tips to help you to recognize them.

TCs are skewed to the negative, highly distorted and largely inferential in nature

When you focus on your adversity at 'A' and hold a set of irrational beliefs about this 'A' then the thinking consequences of these beliefs tend to be inferences. If you recall from Chapter 6, inferences are hunches about events that go beyond the data at hand. They may be correct or distorted and need to be tested against the available information. Inferences occur at 'A' in the 'ABC' and in TCs at 'C'. When these TCs stem from irrational beliefs, these inferences tend to be much more skewed to the negative and much more distorted than the inferences that occur at 'A'. Remember this point as you work to identify your TCs of irrational beliefs and when differentiating between inferences at 'A' and inferences at 'C'.

TCs are characterized by a number of thinking errors that are based on implicit irrational beliefs

David Burns (1980) wrote a self-help book on Cognitive Therapy, in which he outlined a number of thinking errors that are most often present in TCs. Let me outline and illustrate five of the most common thinking errors. As you will see, these TCs are highly distorted interpretations or inferences.

I will begin by describing each thinking error and then I will illustrate each error twice. First, I will illustrate the thinking error as it often appears in your thinking (i.e. without the underpinning irrational belief). Then, I will illustrate and show how each error actually stems from an underlying irrational belief, which appears in square brackets in the second of the illustrations. In both illustrations I will underline the thinking error.

Let me reiterate that as the underlying irrational beliefs are implicit in your thinking, they may well not appear in your conscious thoughts and have to be looked for just beneath the surface of your conscious awareness.

Jumping to unwarranted conclusions

Description: Here, when something bad happens, you make a negative interpretation and treat this as a fact even though there is no definite evidence that convincingly supports your conclusions.

Illustration without irrational belief: 'Since they have seen me fail, <u>they will view me as an incompetent worm</u>.'

Illustration with irrational belief: 'Since they have seen me fail ... [as I absolutely should not have done] ... <u>they will view me as an incompetent worm</u>.'

All-or-none thinking

Description: Here, you use non-overlapping black and white categories.

Illustration without irrational belief: 'If I fail at any important task, <u>I will only ever fail again</u>.'

Illustration with irrational belief: 'If I fail at any important task ... [as I must not do] ... I will only ever fail again.'

Overgeneralization

Description: Here, when something bad happens, you make a generalization from this experience that goes far beyond the data at hand.

Illustration without irrational belief: 'If my boss does not like me, <u>it follows that nobody at work will like me.</u>'

Illustration with irrational belief: '[My boss must like me.] If my boss does not like me, <u>it follows that nobody at work will like me.</u>'

Mind reading

Description: Here, you arbitrarily conclude that someone is reacting negatively to you, and you don't bother to check this out. You regard your thought as a fact.

Illustration without irrational belief: 'I made some errors in the PowerPoint presentation and, <u>when I looked at my boss, I thought he was thinking how hopeless I was and therefore he did think this.</u>'

Illustration with irrational belief: 'I made some errors in the PowerPoint presentation ... [that I absolutely should not have made] ... and <u>when I looked at my boss, I thought he was thinking how hopeless I was and therefore he did think this.</u>'

Always-and-never thinking

Description: Here, when something bad happens, you conclude of living that it will always happen and/or the good alternative will never occur.

Illustration without irrational belief: 'Because my present conditions of living are not good, <u>they'll always be this way and I'll never have any happiness.</u>'

Illustration with irrational belief: 'Because my present conditions of living are not good ... [and they are actually intolerable because they must be better than they are] ... <u>it follows that they'll always be this way and I'll never have any happiness.</u>'

TCs are thoughts that often accompany unhealthy negative emotions that are particularly relevant to the adversity at 'A'

When you are actually experiencing an unhealthy negative emotion (UNE) and you attend to the thinking that accompanies it, then these thoughts are likely to be TCs of irrational beliefs, the content of which is related to the adversity at 'A'. As they are TCs of irrational beliefs, this content is highly distorted and skewed to the negative.

How to formulate realistic and balanced alternatives to thinking consequences of irrational beliefs

Before you respond to the thinking consequences of irrational beliefs, you need to formulate realistic alternatives to these TCs. The first step in doing this is to understand what are the realistic alternatives to the thinking errors listed and illustrated earlier in this chapter. The nature of these alternatives is that they are realistic (i.e. reflect accurately the nature of what has happened, is happening or may happen in the future) and they are balanced (i.e. they incorporate a variety of features – positive, negative and neutral). Table 9.1 provides such a handy list.

Table 9.1 Twelve thinking errors and their realistic and balanced alternatives.

Thinking error	Realistic and balanced alternative
Jumping to unwarranted conclusions	Sticking to the facts and testing out your hunches
All-or-none thinking	Multi-category thinking
Overgeneralization	Making a realistic generalization
Focusing on the negative	Focusing on the complexity of experiences
Disqualifying the positive	Incorporating the positive into a complex view of your experiences
Mind reading	Owning and checking one's thoughts about the reactions of others

Thinking error	Realistic and balanced alternative
Fortune-telling	Owning and checking one's thoughts about what will happen in the future
Always-and-never thinking	Balanced thinking about the past, present and future
Magnification	Keeping things in realistic perspective
Minimization	Using the same balanced perspective for self and others
Emotional reasoning	Sound reasoning based on thinking and feeling
Personalization	Making a realistic attribution

How to respond to thinking consequences of irrational beliefs

There are basically three major ways to respond to the thinking consequences of irrational beliefs:

1 Use them to identify and respond to underlying irrational beliefs.
2 Consider the evidence for and against the TCs and their realistic and balanced alternatives.
3 Acknowledge the existence of the TCs but do not engage with them.

I will now consider these in greater depth.

Use the TCs to identify and respond to your irrational belief, then develop and rehearse the rational belief alternative

As inferences that are highly distorted and skewed to the negative are likely to be thinking consequences (TCs) of irrational beliefs, then one way of responding to them is to trace them back to the irrational belief and respond to this belief. There are a number of ways in which you can do this:

1 If you have time, do a written 'ABC' assessment of the episode in which you had the TCs (see Chapter 6). In doing so, seek to identify and respond to your irrational belief and develop the rational belief alternative. Then, rehearse this rational belief and if you have sufficient conviction in this rational belief then the TCs of your irrational belief will change and become more realistic and balanced. If not, then you may need to deliberately think in ways that are consistent with your developing rational belief. This involves you having previously formulated a realistic and balanced alternative to your highly distorted TCs of irrational beliefs.

2 If you do not have time to do a written 'ABC' of the episode, but you know what you are disturbing yourself about in the episode (i.e. you know what your 'A' is), then use your TCs to ask yourself the question: What demand am I making about this 'A' that has led to these TCs? Once you have formulated this irrational belief, respond to it and rehearse and develop your new rational belief, deliberately focusing on the consequent realistic and balanced TCs of this rational belief if needed (see point 1).

3 If you do not have time to do a written 'ABC' of the episode, and you do not know what you are disturbing yourself about in the episode (i.e. you do not know what your 'A' is), then use your TCs to ask yourself the question: What demand am I making in this situation that has led to these TCs? Then respond to this irrational belief, and rehearse and develop your new rational belief, again deliberately focusing on the consequent realistic and balanced TCs of this rational belief if you need to (see point 1 above).

Consider the evidence of the TCs and their realistic alternatives

Once you have identified the TCs of your irrational belief and formulated more realistic and balanced alternatives, stand back and consider each pair one at a time. Ask yourself the question: Which of these two thoughts best reflects the reality of the situation that I am in, the relevant details in my past and what may happen in the future?

I want to stress one important thing here. It is best to answer this question once you have identified and responded to your irrational belief and developed and rehearsed your alternative rational belief. In other words, you need to be in a reasonably rational frame of mind to answer the aforementioned question objectively. If you consider the question while in an irrational frame of mind, then you will easily find evidence to support your highly distorted TCs and to contradict the realistic and balanced TCs.

Acknowledge the existence of the TCs, but do not engage with them

Even if you use both the methods outlined above, you may still find that your highly distorted TCs come to mind. This is perfectly natural for two main reasons. First, you have probably had more experience thinking the TCs of irrational beliefs than the realistic and balanced TCs of rational beliefs. Second, emotionally charged TCs of irrational beliefs take quite a long time to fade even if you do not engage with them. If you engage with them after using the two approaches to TCs outlined above, you will more likely keep them in your mind rather than dismiss them from your mind.

You may continually engage with these TCs for a number of reasons:

1 You may wish to get rid of these thoughts and think that continually engaging with the thoughts will lead you to be thoroughly convinced that they are not realistic and that this thorough conviction will get rid of them. You are wrong on two counts. First, it is not likely that you will become thoroughly convinced that highly distorted TCs are false in a short period of time. Rather, you need to slowly increase your conviction in their falseness, bit by bit

in small, time-limited chunks. Second, if you try to get rid of thoughts then you will only succeed in keeping them alive. There is a famous psychological experiment that shows that if you are asked to think of a white polar bear and then instruct yourself to dismiss this thought from your mind, then you will, in fact, keep this thought in your mind.

2 You may continually engage with highly distorted TCs because you are demanding certainty. If there is only a small chance that an unlikely, but highly negative, outcome will occur, this is not good enough for you. You need, or more accurately you believe you need, 100-percent certainty that this outcome will not happen and you will search in your mind for ways of achieving such certainty. This cognitive searching for certainty will result only in you keeping highly distorted TCs in your mind.

How can you acknowledge but not engage with highly distorted TCs?

I suggested at the outset of this section that once you have done some work on highly distorted TCs (i.e. by responding to the underlying irrational belief and by considering evidence for and against them), then you need to acknowledge their existence but not engage with them. This is what I mean by this:

What is meant by acknowledgement of TCs?

By acknowledgement of TCs, I mean that you notice the existence of these thoughts and recognize that they are highly distorted TCs of irrational beliefs. You accept, but do not like, the fact that these thoughts are in your mind and that they will stay in your mind until they are not in your mind.

What is meant by non-engagement with TCs?

You can best understand non-engagement with the highly distorted TCs of irrational beliefs by first understanding what it means to engage with them. There are two forms of engagement with TCs: deliberate engagement and unwitting engagement.

* In *deliberate engagement* with TCs, you actively think about the thought and how to prevent it from becoming reality, for example. Thus, if your TC is 'Everyone will laugh at me if I make a mistake', engaging with this thought involves you thinking, for example, (a) what you can do to prevent yourself from making a mistake and (b) how to respond when people are laughing at you.

* In *unwitting engagement* with TCs, you are actively trying not to engage with the thought. Paradoxically, this has the effect that you are, in fact, engaging with it, but are not wishing to do so. Thus, if you decide to watch TV in order to distract yourself from your TCs, then you will fail since as we have seen above, the more you try not to think about something, the more you will tend to think about it. Indeed in unwitting engagement, you are engaged with thinking about what you can do so that you don't think about the TCs!

Non-engagement with highly distorted TCs of irrational beliefs involves you getting on with life as you would if they were not in your mind. Thus, if you were planning to watch a TV programme, do so even though the TCs may still be in your mind. This is different from the above in that you are not trying to distract yourself from your TCs. You acknowledge the fact that they may be in your mind (see previous section), but you get on with whatever you have decided to get on with regardless of their presence (or absence). As you do so, accept, but do not like, that your enjoyment or concentration may be impaired to some degree by the presence of these thoughts.

People report that the effect of such acknowledgement and non-engagement is that the TCs are less present in their mind than when they engage with them or try to get rid of them.

Some useful analogies

Here are two useful analogies that people have found helpful when practising non-engaged acknowledgement of highly distorted TCs:

The radio analogy

'When I have very distorted thoughts, I know that they are coming from my irrational beliefs, so I think of them as voices that are on the radio. I can actively listen to them or not listen to them. The second involves them being there, but if I get on with stuff, I then soon forget that they are there. As soon as I am aware that they are not there though, they come back. But when this happens I just accept this and get on with stuff even though the radio is on.'

The light bulb analogy

'I explain it like this. Imagine that you stare at a lit light bulb and then close your eyes. What happens? You will still have images of the light bulb on your retina which will take a while to fade. If you accept that this is natural and go about your business, you will eventually note that the image of the light bulb has gone. However, if you keep returning to gaze at the light bulb, you will restimulate the retina with its image, thus keeping it alive longer on your retina.'

You are now ready to go back and take another look at the adversity at 'A' which I previously encouraged you to assume was true and to proceed accordingly. This will be the focus of the next chapter.

10

coming back to 'A'

I explained earlier why it was important for you to assume temporarily that 'A' was true and why you should not challenge 'A' until you have identified and questioned your irrational beliefs at 'B'. I will show you in this chapter that the best time to come back to 'A' is when you are in a rational frame of mind about the episode in question, which you should be at this point of the REBT process. When you come to use different ways of re-examining 'A', you will be making an objective consideration of the available evidence in the context of the inference you originally made at 'A' and other possible inferences you could have made. I will also make the point that you can often not determine the truth about 'A'. You can only accept the 'best bet' about what happened given the available evidence.

As stated in Chapter 6, it is important to assume for the time being that the main inference that you made at 'A' in the specific example of your target problem is correct. Doing so will enable you to concentrate on the irrational beliefs underlying your emotional problem. Dealing effectively with 'B' helps you to be in the right frame of mind to stand back and review the main inference that you made at 'A' and to begin to plan to change problematic elements of the situation you found yourself in, if relevant.

Also, as your disturbed feelings originate largely from your irrational belief about 'A' rather than from 'A' itself, your attempts to reconsider this 'A', while holding an irrational belief about it, will be affected by this belief and any reconsideration of the distorted inference you may have made at 'A' will probably be short-lived. As already pointed out, having progressed in changing your irrational belief about 'A', you are likely to be in a more objective frame of mind and it is this that best facilitates accurate re-examination of 'A'.

How to re-examine 'A'

How therefore do you go about reconsidering 'A'? You will need to return to it and ask yourself whether or not this was the most realistic way of regarding the situation. This does not imply that you can know for sure that your 'A' was true or false, for there is rarely any single correct, absolute and agreed way of viewing an event. What it does mean, however, is that you can assess all the evidence available to you about the situation and formulate what may well be the 'best bet' about what has occurred.

In the next sections I suggest ways to examine 'A' to determine whether or not it was the most realistic way of viewing what happened in the situation in which you disturbed yourself.

Considering all relevant possibilities and choosing the most likely one

Look again at your 'ABC' and consider what you wrote under the heading 'Situation'. Then consider whether what you listed under 'A' was the most realistic approach to the situation, taking into account all the evidence at your command. This involves reviewing the inference that you made that forms 'A', considering other inferences, weighing up the possibilities and finally making a choice on the most realistic inference.

Other ways of re-examining 'A'

Here are some alternative ways to re-examine 'A'. You can ask yourself:

* 'How likely is it that "A" happened (or might happen)?'
* 'Would an objective jury agree that "A" happened or might happen? If not, what would the jury's verdict be?'
* 'Did I view (am I viewing) the situation realistically? If not, how could I have viewed (can I view) it more realistically?'
* 'If I asked someone whom I could trust to give me an objective opinion about the truth or falsity of my inference about the situation at hand, what would the person say to me and why? How would this person encourage me to view the situation instead?'
* 'If a friend had told me that she had faced (was facing or was about to face) the same situation as I faced and had made the same inference, what would I say to her about the validity of her inference and why? How would I encourage the person to view the situation instead?'

If, having repeatedly used such methods to reconsider 'A', it appears that you continue to make the same distorted inferences at 'A', then it is likely that you are doing so because you hold a relevant core irrational belief which accounts for your making these distorted inferences. I will examine the issue of core irrational beliefs in Chapter 11.

I have now covered the nuts and bolts of addressing your target problem. I will now consider how you can use these and other related skills across the board.

11

using established and new skills across the board

If you have several problems, then you can use your recurring unhealthy negative emotions and the specific 'A's' you have assessed in your 'Situational ABC' forms to identify recurring themes at 'A'. In such cases, it is likely you hold core irrational beliefs about these general themes and I will show you how to identify these and to develop core rational alternative beliefs. You need to question both, using your established questioning skills but focusing on arguments you find particularly persuasive. Once you have done this, I will show you how to strengthen your core rational beliefs using more general versions of the methods I taught you in Chapter 8. I will also explain how your core irrational beliefs combine with the principle of uncertainty to form distorted inferences at 'A' and will help you to correct any biases you find in your thinking there.

There is much more to REBT than helping you to deal with specific examples of your emotional problems. In this chapter, then, I will show you how to apply these and other related skills more widely.

Identifying recurring themes at 'A'

Once you have worked through a number of specific examples of your emotional problems, you may realize that you tend to disturb yourself about similar things. Put differently there may be recurring themes at 'A' in the 'ABC' framework. There are two ways of identifying such themes.

Use your emotion

If your problems are reflected by a given problematic emotion, then this emotion has one theme or a small number of themes associated with it. I have presented the eight unhealthy negative emotions and the major themes associated with them in Table 3.1.

Using emotions to identify themes will only provide you with general themes and not necessarily their specific content. For this you need to consult the 'As' of your 'Situational ABC' forms as discussed below.

Identifying core irrational beliefs and core rational beliefs

In this section, I will consider core irrational beliefs and their core rational belief alternatives.

Core irrational beliefs

A core irrational belief is a general irrational belief that you hold about a recurring theme and which explains why you are disturbed in many situations where that theme is present or where you think that it is present.

Like a specific irrational belief, a core irrational belief comprises a rigid belief and one major extreme belief (i.e. an awfulizing belief, a discomfort intolerance belief or a depreciation belief).

Here are some useful guidelines concerning the nature of core irrational beliefs and types of emotional problems:

1 Core irrational beliefs in self-esteem problems (including shame and guilt) involve a rigid belief and a self-depreciation belief (e.g. 'When I am involved in a situation, I must make sure that nobody gets hurt and if I don't then I am a bad person').

2 Core irrational beliefs in many forms of unhealthy anger involve a rigid belief and an other-depreciation belief (e.g. 'Other people must not try to take advantage of me and if they do they are evil').

3 Core irrational beliefs in non-ego anxiety that features highly exaggerated thinking consequences involve a rigid demand and an awfulizing belief (e.g. 'I must be in control of myself and it will be awful if I begin to lose such control').

4 Core irrational beliefs in self-discipline problems involve a rigid demand and a discomfort intolerance belief (e.g. 'Before I get down to any work I must feel like doing it and I can't bear the discomfort of doing things when I don't feel like doing so').

Core rational beliefs

A core rational belief is a general rational belief that you hold about a recurring theme and which explains your constructive response in the many situations where that theme is present or where you think that it is present.

Like a specific rational belief, a core rational belief comprises a flexible belief and one major non-extreme belief (i.e. a non-awfulizing belief, a discomfort tolerance belief or an acceptance belief).

Here are some useful guidelines concerning the nature of core rational beliefs and types of healthy responses to adversities:

1 Core rational beliefs in healthy responses to self-esteem problems involve a flexible belief and a self-acceptance belief (e.g. 'When I am involved in a situation, I want to make sure that nobody gets hurt, but sadly I don't have to do so. If I don't then I am not a bad person; I am a fallible human being with responsibility over my own behaviour in such situations, but with no responsibility over how other people act').

2 Core rational beliefs in healthy responses to anger-related themes involve a flexible belief and an other-acceptance belief (e.g. 'I don't want other people to try to take advantage of me, but that does not mean that they must not try. If they do, they are fallible and are acting badly and not evil').

3 Core rational beliefs in healthy responses to non-ego anxiety that features highly exaggerated cognitive consequences involve a flexible belief and a non-awfulizing belief (e.g. 'I want to be in control of myself, but I don't have to be in such control. It will be bad if I begin to lose such control, but it would not be awful').

4 Core rational beliefs in healthy responses to self-discipline problems involve a flexible belief and a discomfort tolerance belief (e.g. 'Before I get down to any work I prefer to feel like doing it, but I don't have to have this feeling. If I don't, it is difficult to bear, but I can bear it').

Questioning core beliefs

Questioning core irrational beliefs and core rational beliefs involves similar skills to questioning specific beliefs.
I suggest that you consult Chapter 7 for a detailed consideration of how to question your beliefs. The main difference between questioning specific beliefs and core beliefs is that when you do the latter you are not constrained by specific situations. When you come to question your beliefs, while it is important to use

questions concerning the truth, logic and pragmatic value of both irrational and rational beliefs, it is perhaps more important for you to use arguments that you find particularly persuasive.

Strengthening core rational beliefs

In Chapter 8 I discussed several ways of strengthening conviction in your specific rational beliefs. The methods I discussed included the attack–response technique, and acting and thinking in ways that are consistent with your developing specific beliefs. You can use these techniques to strengthen your conviction in your core rational beliefs.

Identifying and responding to recurring highly distorted inferences at 'C'

You will recall that in the 'Situational ABC' model of psychological disturbance and health that I have used in this book, 'C' stands for the thinking consequences of irrational or rational beliefs. I have argued that the thinking consequences of specific irrational beliefs tend to be highly distorted and unrealistic and this is also the case when we consider the thinking consequences of core irrational beliefs.

There are a number of ways to deal with recurring highly distorted inferences at 'C' and in what follows I will consider them (see also Chapter 9).

Identify the recurring highly distorted inferences

In Chapter 9 I discussed what constitutes a highly distorted inference. To recap, an inference is a thought that goes beyond the data at hand. It may be accurate or inaccurate. A highly distorted inference is a thought that goes well beyond the data at hand and involves you thinking in very exaggerated and negative ways. As such, highly distorted inferences are very likely to be inaccurate. Thus, if you believe that you must not make a mistake in public and that if you do 'everybody will criticize me', then this latter thought is highly distorted in that it predicts that all the people present will respond in a negative way. This is unlikely to be true unless your mistake is so bad to occasion such a response from everybody present.

So far, I have discussed highly distorted thoughts at 'C'. However, you may also think in pictures and these images may also be highly distorted in nature. Thus, rather than have the verbally based thought 'everybody will criticize me', you may have an image where you see in your mind's eye everybody present criticizing you for the mistake that you made.

If you notice that you routinely have such highly distorted thoughts or images, then there are a number of ways of dealing with them which I will now discuss.

Go back to your core irrational belief (CIB) and question it

The existence of recurring highly distorted thoughts and images at 'C' indicates that your core irrational belief is active and needs to be questioned. Thus, you can use the presence of these highly distorted cognitions to go back to 'B' and briefly question your CIB and ensure that your core rational belief (CRB) is in place.

When you return to 'B' at this point, please note that your goal is not to completely convince yourself of the rationality of your CRB and of the irrationality of your CIB, but to take a step towards this outcome. Think of conviction as being on a 0–100-per-cent continuum (as used in the attack–response technique described in Chapter 8 and earlier in this chapter).

Identify the thinking error(s) in your recurring highly distorted inferences

In Chapter 9 I discussed the major errors that you make when your inferences at 'C' are highly distorted. These are known as thinking errors and, if you need to, I suggest that you review this material at this point. It is useful for you to note the thinking error and appreciate what it is about your subsequent thinking that is distorted.

Develop realistic and balanced alternatives to your recurring highly distorted inferences

It is important that you develop realistic and balanced alternatives to your recurring highly distorted inferences. If you do not do so, then you will tend to continue to think in such highly distorted ways, given that you have no alternative thoughts to think.

When to respond to your recurring highly distorted inferences and engage with realistic and balanced thinking

Much of CBT is based on the principle that when you identify your distorted thinking it is important that you examine and respond to it and think healthily instead. Thus, when you identify your recurring highly distorted thinking that stems from your core irrational beliefs, it is important that you respond to it and engage with the realistic and balanced alternatives. However, there are exceptions to this principle which I will detail below.

When not to respond to your recurring highly distorted inferences nor engage with realistic and balanced thinking

When you have done some work at questioning your core beliefs and have responded to your recurring highly distorted inferences that stem from your core irrational beliefs, you may well find that you still have these highly distorted thoughts in your mind even though you are developing your core rational beliefs.

I liken this phenomenon to staring at a light bulb and then closing your eyes. When you do this you will still see the light as an after image on your retina. The best way to deal with this is to accept it and don't go back to look at the light.

In the same way, when your highly distorted thoughts remain in your mind despite your efforts to respond to them and to the core irrational beliefs that underpin them, then these are what I call 'cognitive reverberations' – thoughts that are equivalent to the reverberating image of the light on your retina. The best way to deal with such thoughts is to acknowledge their existence, understand that they are reverberating thoughts and don't engage with them. Rather, pursue your goals while such thoughts stay in your mind. If you allow yourself to do this then these thoughts will go far more quickly than if you re-engage with them, distract yourself from them or attempt to suppress them.

Why you make distorted inferences at 'As'

As you will recall, when you are working on a specific example of your problem using the 'ABC' framework, it is important that you begin by assuming temporarily that your adversity at 'A' is correct, even though it may seem distorted. Doing so will help you to identify your irrational beliefs at 'B' which, according to REBT, are at the root of your emotional problems. If you corrected the distortion at 'A' at the outset, then you would not be motivated to identify, question and change your irrational beliefs at 'B'. As such, you would be vulnerable to disturbance as your irrational beliefs would remain unchallenged.

As I discussed in Chapter 10, the time to question your 'A', if it seems distorted, is after you have questioned your beliefs at 'B' and are committed to strengthening your rational beliefs. Once you have done this, the following question remains: Why do you make distorted inferences at 'A'?

Here is how REBT explains this process. We have seen that, when you disturb yourself across a range of similar situations, it is because you hold a core irrational belief. Now you tend to bring your core beliefs to situations which are related to themes about which you disturb yourself. Thus, if your core irrational belief is 'I must not be criticized by authority figures', then you will tend to bring this belief to situations where there is a possibility of you being criticized by authority figures.

To this scenario, let's add the concept of uncertainty, in particular not knowing that the adversity at 'A' will not happen. When you add this type of uncertainty to your core irrational belief (e.g. 'I must not be criticized by authority figures'), then this core belief is modified to incorporate uncertainty (i.e. 'I must know that the authority figures will not criticize me'). When you bring this core belief to situations where there is uncertainty about whether or not you will be criticized by authority figures, then, unless you can convince yourself that these figures will not criticize you, you will tend to think that they *will* criticize you. When you do that, you have created a distorted inference at 'A'. This is shown in Figure 11.1.

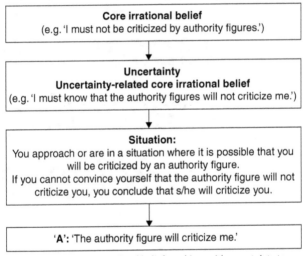

Figure 11.1 *How a core irrational belief combines with uncertainty to create a distorted inference at 'A'.*

You can use this information to correct any biases you have when you make inferences at 'A'. However, remember to continue to identify and respond to your irrational beliefs at 'B'.

In Chapter 13 I will discuss how you can maintain and enhance the gains that you have made so far. But first I will consider how you can deal with lapses and prevent relapse.

12

dealing with lapses and preventing relapse

Lapses are an inevitable part of the change process and the best way to deal with lapses is to first develop rational beliefs about them. In order to prevent relapse, you need to deal with and learn from your lapses. In this chapter, I will show you how to prevent relapse by identifying and dealing effectively with your vulnerability factors. Here, you need to prepare yourself to face your vulnerability factors by using the 'Situational ABC' framework and through imagery. When you face your vulnerability factors, use the 'challenging, but not overwhelming' concept and rehearse relevant rational beliefs before and during the experience. As with lapses, it is best to develop rational beliefs about relapse. If you do, you are less likely to relapse than you would if you held irrational beliefs about it. If you do relapse, first un-disturb yourself about this grim reality and then learn from it.

Once you have made progress in overcoming your problems and you have used your REBT skills across the board, you need to deal with lapses to continue progress and thus help yourself to prevent relapse. A lapse is a temporary and non-serious return to a problem state while a relapse is a more enduring, serious return to that state. In order to help yourself to prevent a relapse you need to use a sequence of steps to do so.

The relapse prevention sequence and how to use it

In using the relapse prevention sequence which I will discuss below, please bear in mind that this sequence and the order in which it is presented are suggestions and you should not follow them slavishly. Use the sequence as a guide and modify it according to your own situation.

Review what you have achieved so far and think through how you can apply what you have learned to future related problems

This initial step in the relapse prevention sequence is related to and builds on the work that you did in the previous chapter. In order to know how to deal with relapse you need to know what you have achieved so far in the REBT process of self-help. It is helpful to go back to your goals and ask yourself to what extent you have achieved them and what you have learned that has enabled you to have made the progress that you have made. Using this knowledge you can begin to think through how you can apply this learning to related problems that you may encounter in the future.

Develop rational beliefs about lapses

I have defined a lapse as a temporary and non-serious return to a problem state. As such, it is very likely that you will experience a number of lapses along the path to personal change.

Despite this, it is important that you develop rational beliefs about experiencing such lapses. Doing so will help you to learn from these lapses. On the other hand, if you hold a set of irrational beliefs about lapsing, then you will disturb yourself about doing so which will both impede you from learning from these lapses and thus increase the chances of experiencing a relapse, which I have defined as a more enduring, serious return to a problem state. What follows is a set of rational beliefs that you can adapt for your own use in thinking about and responding to the inevitable lapses along the way to personal change:

* I would prefer not to experience lapses, but I am not immune from them and nor do I have to be.
* It is unfortunate to experience lapses, but not the end of the world.
* It is a struggle to put up with lapsing, but I can tolerate it and it is worth it to me to do so.
* I am a fallible human being who experiences lapses along the way to personal change. I am not less of a person for doing so.
* The world is not a rotten place for allowing lapses to occur. It is a complex mixture of the good, the bad and the neutral.

If you develop such a rational philosophy then you will be best placed to deal with the main reason why people relapse – failure to deal with factors that render them particularly vulnerable to lapsing.

Identify factors to which you remain vulnerable

As I have just said, vulnerability factors are factors that if you encounter them render you vulnerable to experiencing your problems once again. A vulnerability factor may be external to you or internal. Typical external vulnerability factors are negative situations involving other people which you find particularly problematic and which are either inherently bound up with your main problems or which have a bearing on them. Thus, if you are trying to give up smoking, being with other people who smoke and who urge you to join them may serve as an external vulnerability factor to you.

Typical internal vulnerability factors include urges, thoughts and a sense of discomfort. For example, if you are working towards greater self-discipline and you experience an urge to do something that will take you away from self-disciplined behaviour, then this constitutes an internal vulnerability factor.

A vulnerability factor may be the same as the 'A' that you originally identified when you were first working on your problems or it may be different, albeit related. The most reliable way of identifying a vulnerability factor is to consider times when you lapsed back into your problem having made progress. If such lapses occurred in situations that were similar, then a vulnerability factor is likely to be present in such situations.

Table 12.1 The application of the 'Situational ABC' framework to the identification of a vulnerability factor.

'Situation'	=	The situation in which the lapse occurred
'A'	=	Vulnerability factor (The aspect of the situation to which you had the unhealthy response)
'B'	=	Irrational beliefs
'C'	=	Unhealthy response

Determine how you would deal constructively with these vulnerability factors

Once you have used the 'Situational ABC' framework to identify your vulnerability factor at 'A', then you can continue to use it to identify and respond to the irrational beliefs at 'B' in dealing with specific examples where you did not deal with your vulnerability factors in constructive ways. You do this in the same way as you did when working on specific examples of your problem (see Chapter 6).

Using imagery rehearsal of rational beliefs

Once you have committed yourself to strengthening the rational beliefs that underpin how you would like to respond emotionally to your vulnerability factor, you need to use some of the strengthening techniques that I discussed in Chapter 8. In particular, you can use rational-emotive imagery as follows:

1 Close your eyes and see yourself facing your vulnerability factor and make yourself feel emotionally disturbed as you do so.
2 While you are still facing the vulnerability factor change your emotional response to the way you would like to feel in relation to the factor (this will be a healthy negative emotion, or HNE) and hold that response for a few minutes.
3 Ensure that you changed your emotional response by changing your irrational beliefs to their rational belief equivalents. If not, repeat the technique until you have done so.

Repeat this exercise three times a day until your emotional response to the vulnerability factor is healthy and negative.

Using imagery rehearsal of constructive behaviour

You can also use imagery to rehearse seeing yourself act in constructive ways when facing your vulnerability factor. Some people find this a very useful step to take before taking action in the face of their actual vulnerability factor, while for others this step is not necessary or is even counterproductive. You might like to try out this technique to determine for yourself whether or not it is likely to be helpful as preparation for taking action in the real world.

If you do decide to use imagery rehearsal to imagine yourself acting constructively in facing your vulnerability factor, then the more vividly you can imagine doing this, the better. However, some people do not have a store of vivid imagery and, if this applies to you, don't worry. You can still use imagery with benefit. Here is what you do:

Select a vulnerability factor that is challenging for you to deal with, but you do not find overwhelming.

1 Be clear with yourself what your vulnerability factor is. This is likely to be the 'A' in the 'Situational ABC' framework.
2 Be clear with yourself how you are going to deal constructively with this vulnerability factor.
3 Choose a situation in which it is likely that you will encounter your vulnerability factor.
4 Get yourself into the right frame of mind by rehearsing your relevant rational beliefs.
5 See yourself facing your vulnerability factor and dealing with it constructively. It is better to see yourself struggle than to see yourself showing unrealistic mastery.

Repeat this imagery exercise three times a day until you are ready to face the vulnerability in reality.

Put this constructive plan into action

You are now ready to face your vulnerability factor armed with your rational beliefs and a clear idea of how you are going to act when you face it. You can use the principle that I have called 'challenging, but not overwhelming' here. In deciding that facing your vulnerability factor in a given context constitutes a challenge for you, but is not overwhelming, you are not, in common parlance, 'biting off more than you can chew' by taking this step. It is useful to get yourself in the right frame of mind by rehearsing your rational belief before you take action and to hold this belief in mind while you are taking action. While the former is almost always possible, the latter is more difficult given that you may have to concentrate fully on what you are doing and may not have time to rehearse your rational belief *in situ*, even briefly. Don't worry if this is the case, since your pre-action rehearsal of your rational belief will often be enough to carry you through and, if not, you can review and learn from this experience later.

Review your experiences

Once you have taken action in the face of your vulnerability factors several times, it is important that you stand back and review your experiences of doing so in order to learn from experiences. Doing so will help you to fine tune your responses to your vulnerability factors.

Develop rational beliefs about relapse

As I mentioned at the beginning of this chapter, a relapse is a more enduring, serious return to a problem, colloquially referred to as 'going back to square one'. So far in this chapter I have discussed the steps that you need to take to deal with lapses and your vulnerability factors and thus help to prevent relapse. However, as it is possible for you to relapse, it is important to face up to and deal with this possibility. Once you have done so, ask yourself what it is about relapsing that you would disturb yourself about. As you will know this represents your 'A' in the 'Situational ABC' framework. In my experience, people disturb themselves about two major 'As': weakness ('If I relapse, it reveals a weakness about me') and loss of self-control ('If I relapse, it means that I have lost self-control').

Develop rational beliefs about weakness-related relapse

When you disturb yourself about relapsing because it reveals a weakness, you tend to experience shame which motivates you to avoid dealing with the possibility of relapse. You tend to think that people will look down on you and dismiss you should you relapse.

If you experience shame about relapsing, it's important that you develop the following rational beliefs which you need to put into your own words:

* *Flexible belief*: 'I really don't want to be weak and relapse, but sadly and regretfully I am not immune from doing so and nor do I have to be so immune.'
* *Non-awfulizing belief*: 'It would be unfortunate if I were to be weak and relapse, but it would not be the end of the world.'

* *Discomfort tolerance belief*: 'It would be a struggle for me to put up with being weak and relapsing, but I could tolerate it and it is worth it to me to do so.'
* *Self-acceptance belief*: 'If I relapse, that would be bad but it would not prove that I am a weak pathetic person. It means that I am a complex, unrateable, fallible human being.'

Develop rational beliefs about relapse related to loss of self-control

When you disturb yourself about relapsing because it indicates that you have experienced a loss of self-control, you tend to experience anxiety which leads you to make a desperate attempt to regain such self-control. However, because your attempt is based on desperation, it leads you to become more anxious rather than less anxious and this increases the negativity of your subsequent thoughts about the extent and implications of such loss of self-control (i.e. your subsequent thinking is highly distorted and skewed to the negative).

If you experience anxiety about the loss of self-control that accompanies relapse, then again it's important that you develop the following rational beliefs which you need to put into your own words:

* *Flexible belief*: 'I really don't want to relapse and lose self-control, but sadly and regretfully I am not immune from doing so and nor do I have to be so immune.'
* *Non-awfulizing belief*: 'It would be unfortunate if I were to relapse and lose self-control, but it would not be the end of the world.'
* *Discomfort tolerance belief*: 'It would be a struggle for me to put up with relapsing and losing self-control, but I could tolerate it and it is worth it to me to do so.'
* *Life-acceptance belief*: 'If I relapse and lose self-control, that would be bad but it would not prove that life is all bad for allowing this to happen to me. Life is a complex mixture of the good, the bad and the neutral.'

Develop rational beliefs about relapse in general

In the above two sections, I have considered two of the most common problems that people tend to have about relapsing (i.e. being weak and losing self-control) and I have outlined the rational beliefs that you need to develop if you experience one or both of these issues. However, some people disturb themselves about the fact of relapse without any surplus meaning and, if this applies to you, it is important that you develop a set of rational beliefs about the fact of relapse. I will list these now, but suggest that you modify them to suit your own situation:

* *Flexible belief*: 'I really don't want to relapse, but sadly and regretfully I am not immune from relapse and nor do I have to be so immune.'
* *Non-awfulizing belief*: 'It would be unfortunate if I were to relapse, but it would not be the end of the world.'
* *Discomfort tolerance belief*: 'It would be a struggle for me to put up with relapsing, but I could tolerate it and it is worth it to me to do so.'
* *Self-acceptance belief*: 'If I relapse, that would be bad but it would not prove that I am a weak pathetic person. It means that I am a complex, unrateable, fallible human being.'
* *Life-acceptance belief*: 'If I relapse, life is not bad. It is a complex place where many good, bad and neutral things happen including relapse.'

Be rational and learn from relapse

If you develop and implement a rational philosophy about relapsing then you will calm down about the prospect of it happening. This will help you to put the likelihood of you relapsing into perspective and help you to realize that you will lessen the chance of doing so if you are diligent in learning from your relapses and if you deal adequately with your vulnerability factors.

In the next chapter I will discuss how you can maintain the gains that you have made in using REBT.

13

maintaining your gains

Once you have made gains at dealing with your emotional problems, it is important that you do not rest on your laurels. If you do so, then you will soon lose the gains that you have made. In this chapter, therefore, I will discuss the importance of taking and applying personal responsibility for actively working to maintain your gains. I will show you that the key to maintaining your gains is to implement the idea that you need to keep thinking rationally about adversities and to keep acting and thinking in ways that are consistent with such rational thinking. I will also outline what the founder of REBT, Dr. Albert Ellis, had to say about maintaining your hard won gains.

As I discussed in Chapter 12, personal change, like the course of true love, rarely runs smoothly. Thus, once you have made progress in addressing your problems, you cannot afford to rest on your laurels. You need to take responsibility for actively maintaining the gains that you have made and even enhancing them if you want to capitalize on the skills that you have learned in this book. In this chapter, then, I will focus on showing you how you can maintain the gains that you have made and the philosophy you need to develop to enable you to deal with obstacles to gain maintenance.

Take responsibility for maintaining your gains

As we have seen, REBT argues that you are largely responsible for whether or not you disturb yourself about adversities at 'A', and you are also largely responsible for maintaining the gains that you have made by using the principles outlined in this book.

In Chapter 12 I discussed how you can deal with lapses to prevent relapsing. In this chapter I will show you, more generally, what you can do to maintain your gains once you have made progress.

How to maintain your gains

More than 25 years ago, Albert Ellis, the founder of REBT, made a number of important suggestions concerning how you can maintain the gains that you have made from using REBT principles and techniques (Ellis 1984). I have borrowed liberally from his ideas in this section. Here are the suggestions:

1 When you have made gains and then begin to backslide into your old problems, remember as precisely as you can what thoughts, feelings and behaviours you once changed to bring about your improvement. If you again feel disturbed, think

back to how you previously used REBT principles to make yourself undisturbed. For example, you may remember that:

* you accepted yourself whenever authority figures criticized you (or you thought that they might) rather than condemning yourself as worthless as you did previously
* you tolerated the discomfort of asking your neighbours to refrain from making a noise, when you had previously thought that you could not bear to do this
* you decided to spend time with your mother-in-law for the sake of your spouse and worked to accept her as a fallible human being for her interfering behaviour.

Remind yourself of the beliefs, thoughts, feelings and behaviours that you have changed and how you changed them. Use that information when you notice that you have begun to backslide.

2 Keep rehearsing rational beliefs or coping statements based on these beliefs, such as: 'It's great to be accepted, but I can fully accept myself as a person and enjoy life considerably even when I am rejected!' Don't merely repeat these statements by rote, but really think them through many times until you really begin to believe and feel that they are true. However, don't over-rehearse such statements.

3 Keep seeking for, discovering and questioning your irrational beliefs with which you are once again disturbing yourself. Take each important irrational belief – such as 'I have to succeed and I am not a worthwhile person if I don't!' – and keep asking yourself: 'Why is this belief true?', 'Where is the evidence that my worth to myself, and my enjoyment of living, utterly depend on my succeeding at something?', 'In what way would I be totally unacceptable as a human if I failed at an important task or test?' Keep questioning your irrational beliefs persistently and persuasively wherever you see that you are letting them creep back again. And even when you don't actively hold

them, realize that they may arise once more; so bring them to your consciousness, and preventatively – and persuasively – dispute them.

Keep risking and doing things that you would normally avoid doing – such as asking people out on a date, job hunting or creative writing. Once you have partly overcome one of your anxieties, keep acting against it on a regular basis. If you feel uncomfortable in forcing yourself to do things that you are unrealistically afraid of doing, don't allow yourself to avoid doing them – thereby preserving your discomfort for ever! Make yourself as uncomfortable as you can be in order to address effectively your irrational fears and to become unanxious and comfortable later.

4 Try to see clearly the difference between healthy negative feelings – such as those of sadness, remorse and disappointment, when you do not get some of the important things you want – and unhealthy negative feelings – such as those of depression, unhealthy guilt and shame under the same circumstances. Realize that you are capable of changing your unhealthy negative feelings to healthy negative ones by changing your rigid and extreme beliefs to their flexible and non-extreme counterparts. Thus, take your depressed feelings and work on them until you feel only sad and sorry. Take your anxious feelings and work on them until you feel only concerned and vigilant. Use the variety of REBT techniques that I have described in this book to do this.

5 Avoid self-defeating procrastination. Do unpleasant tasks fast – today! If you still procrastinate, reward yourself with certain things that you enjoy – for example, reading and socializing – only after you have performed the tasks that you easily avoid. If this won't work, give yourself a severe penalty – such as talking to a person whom you find boring for two hours or giving away a £20 note to an unworthy cause – every time that you procrastinate.

6 Show yourself that it is an absorbing challenge and something of an adventure to maintain your emotional health and to keep yourself reasonably happy no matter what kind of misfortunes assail you. Make the uprooting of your misery one of the most important things in your life – something you are utterly determined to steadily work at achieving. Fully acknowledge that you almost always have some choice about how to think, feel and behave, and throw yourself actively into making that choice for yourself.

7 Remember – and use – the three main insights of REBT:
* *Insight 1*: You largely choose to disturb yourself about the unpleasant events of your life, although you may be encouraged to do so by external happenings and by social learning. You mainly feel the way you think. When obnoxious and frustrating things happen to you at point 'A' (adversity), you consciously or unconsciously select rational beliefs that lead you to feel concerned, sad and remorseful and you also select irrational beliefs that lead you to feel anxious, depressed and guilty.
* *Insight 2*: No matter how or when you acquired your irrational beliefs and your self-sabotaging habits, you now, in the present, choose to maintain them – and that is why you are now disturbed. Your past history and your present life conditions importantly affect you; but they don't disturb you. Your present philosophy is the main contributor to your current disturbance.
* *Insight 3*: There is no magical way for you to change your strong tendencies needlessly to upset yourself. However, you can minimize the impact of these tendencies through persistent work and practice to enable you to alter your irrational beliefs, your unhealthy feelings and your self-destructive behaviours.

8 Try to keep in touch with several other people who know something about REBT who can help go over some of its aspects with you. Tell them about problems that you have

difficulty coping with and let them know how you are using REBT principles to overcome these problems. See if they agree with your solutions and ask them to suggest additional and better kinds of questioning methods that you can use to work against your irrational beliefs.

9 Practise using REBT methods with some of your friends, relatives and associates who are willing to let you try to help them with it. The more often you use it with others, and are able to see what their irrational beliefs are and to try to talk them out of these self-defeating ideas, the more you will be able to understand the main principles of REBT and to use them for yourself. When you see other people act irrationally and in a disturbed manner, try to figure out – with or without talking to them about it – what their main irrational beliefs probably are and how these could be actively and vigorously disputed.

10 Keep going back to REBT reading and audiovisual material from time to time, to keep reminding yourself of some of the main REBT principles and philosophies.

11 Remember and use the following philosophy concerning how to deal with obstacles to maintaining the gains you have made.

Develop and implement a philosophy of dealing with obstacles to maintaining your gains

In this section I want to stress the importance of developing and implementing a philosophy of dealing with obstacles to maintaining the gains you have made.

It would be nice to think that when you have made progress at achieving your personal goals, then you have done all the hard work that you need to do in the change process. Sadly, this is not the case. How many times have you succeeded at losing weight, for example, only to relax your efforts and put that weight back later? Mark Twain once said, 'Giving up smoking is easy, I've done it hundreds of times!' I have already pointed out that it is highly likely that you will experience lapses in your progress and, if you don't identify and deal effectively with your vulnerability factors, then you will increase your chances of relapsing.

When I talk of a philosophy of dealing with obstacles to maintaining the gains you have made, I mean the following:

* Recognize that you will continue to experience obstacles to maintaining the changes you have made throughout the change process.
* Refrain from demanding that this not be the case. Rather, accept, but do not like, this undesirable state of affairs.
* Resolve to use the 'Situational ABC' framework to assess obstacles to maintaining progress whenever you encounter them.
* Identify and examine any irrational beliefs that you discover which account for your obstacles.
* Construct, develop and rehearse rational alternatives to these irrational beliefs.Act and think in ways that are in keeping with these rational beliefs as you confront the obstacles at 'A'.
* Once you have done this go back to 'A' to re-examine it. If it is distorted, correct the distortion.
* Identify, challenge and change any core irrational beliefs that you hold which explain why you may perceive obstacles at 'A' that in reality are not there.
* Develop, rehearse and strengthen through action alternative core rational beliefs and see the effect that doing so has on the inferences that you make at 'A'.
* Make the practice of the self-help methods of REBT an integral part of your ongoing response to any obstacles that you encounter and of your future self-care regime.

'SITUATION' =

'A' =

'iB' (irrational belief) =   **'rB' (rational belief) =**

'C' (emotional consequence) =   **'C' (emotional goal) =**

'C' (behavioural consequence) =   **'C' (behavioural goal) =**

'C' (thinking consequence) =   **'C' (thinking goal) =**

1 Write down a brief, objective description of the 'situation'.
2 Identify your 'C' – your major disturbed emotion, dysfunctional behaviour and, if relevant, distorted subsequent thinking.
3 Identify your 'A' – this is what you were most disturbed about in the situation (Steps 2 and 3 are interchangeable).
4 Set emotional, behavioural and thinking goals.
5 Identify irrational beliefs ('iBs') i.e. rigid belief plus one of the following extreme beliefs: awfulizing belief, discomfort intolerance or depreciation belief (self, others or life).
6 Identify alternative rational beliefs ('rBs') to enable you to achieve your goals i.e. flexible belief plus one of the following non-extreme beliefs: non-awfulizing belief, discomfort tolerance or acceptance belief (self, others or life).

Lightning Source UK Ltd.
Milton Keynes UK
UKHW021849211021
392618UK00005B/188